Project 1-Benson

Rhythm Project: Grades: 2–3

Repertoire: *Mouse, Mousie* Traditional singing game
              #20 Erstes Spiel am Xylophon Gunild Keetman
              Lizard in My Soup K. Benson

Lesson Developer: Karen K. Benson

Making Music
Students play singing game *Mouse, Mousie*

Mouse, Mous - ie   in   the   hous - ie   Hur - ry,   hur - ry   do.

Or   the   kit - ty   in   the   hous - ie   will   be   chas - ing   you.

Game: In a standing circle with hands connected, the "kitty" walks around the outside of the circle while the "mouse" is inside the circle. At the end of the song, arms are lifted creating windows for the mouse to escape. If the mouse can run around the outside of the circle and return through the same window without being caught by the cat, they win and get to be the next cat and a new mouse is chosen. If caught, a new mouse is chosen and play continues.

Students identify the rhythmic building blocks found in the text rhythm of *Mouse, Mousie*

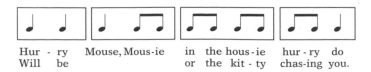

Hur - ry	Mouse, Mous-ie	in the hous-ie	hur - ry do
Will be		or the kit - ty	chas-ing you.

Students create melodies using rhythmic building blocks

At xylophones set in C pentatonic, students explore playing rhythmic building blocks creating melodic ideas and patterns. One strategy to try is to have students play the patterns on one pitch, then two pitches, then three, etc. Next, begin to combine two blocks to make longer rhythmic ideas. As time allows, patterns can be combined that reflect elemental phrase structures such as ABAB, ABAC, etc.

To make the melodic phrases sound complete, ask the students to finish their new melodies on tonic (C, in this instance).

Students transfer the rhythmic building blocks to play *#20 Erstes Spiel am Xylophon*

- Students begin reading the rhythm to *#20 Erstes Spiel* from visual. Once secure, students play the rhythm only on "G". During each repetition, modify the melody, adding pitches until the complete melody is learned. Consider adding a simple chord drone (C and G) on the downbeat.

The completed melody can serve as the A section with student melodies serving as contrasting sections. Student melodies can also be accompanied with the drone simple chord drone.

#20 Erstes Spiel am Xylophon

Making Up Music

Students learn poem, *Lizard in My Soup*

> Live lizard, dead lizard
> Marinated, fried
> Poached lizard, pickled lizard
> Salty lizard hide

Students identify words that relate to the poem and correspond to the rhythmic building blocks

Liz - ard　　Live　liz - ard　Pick-led　liz - ard　Liz - ard hide　Salt　　Fried

- Students create 8-beat "menus" by developing and combining other odd or strange items that relate to the lizard dinner theme.

  Example:

bird　feath - ers,　creep - y　crawl - ies,　spi - der　eggs,　frog　legs.

Students create 8-beat "menu" melodies

Transfer the student created 8-beat "menu" rhythms to xylophone explorations in E *la*-based pentatonic. Refine improvisations into melodic phrases. This can lead to a class performance with the following:

1. Students speak poem text while playing text rhythm on E accompanied by simple drone for A section.
2. Students play menu improvisations for B sections.

Making Sense of Music

Given individual sets of rhythmic building blocks, students notate rhythms presented through body percussion or played on a non-pitched percussion instrument by the teacher or work partner. Students then arrange the blocks to show the rhythmic notation of the pattern. Start with simple 2 and 4 beat patterns based on the rhythmic building blocks and gradually increase phrase length to 8 beats by combining bricks to extend the pattern.

Students complete the sentence prompt "I understand the rhythmic building blocks because…" in a journal. Students copy their own rhythmic compositions into the journal adding text when desired.

Reflection

The purpose of this lesson was to review simple duple rhythm patterns known as rhythmic building blocks with my 3rd grade students. In choosing selections for the *Artful* portion of this lesson, I turned to the traditional singing game "Mouse Mousie" that also contained most of the rhythmic building block patterns. The singing game had been played in 2nd grade. This made the learning process go quickly since the material was already internalized for most of the students. New students and those who needed additional practice rapidly caught up with their peers because of the repetitive nature of the game. *#20 in Erstes Spiel am Xylophon*, contained the same rhythmic elements and is set with a simple melody that easily transferred to xylophone playing because the children had internalized the rhythms.

 Making rhythmic connections with word syllables helps my students grasp rhythm concepts and also reinforces reading skills. For the *Playful* portion of this lesson, I selected the first stanza of the poem "Witches' Menu." This engaging text became the basis for exploration and creating with the rhythmic building blocks. The students enjoyed developing and performing their new phrases for the class. To extend the activity, the class improvised melodies on soprano recorders based on the rhythm of the poem text.

 Selecting the *Mindful* activity comes down to what my students love doing, making music. Using small sets of the rhythmic building blocks, students could compose, read, and perform the rhythms independently. They are now more skilled at aural and visual identification of these rhythms in music utilized in our classroom. Some children went a step further and notated their compositions so they could keep them.

 Many aspects of Frazee's model were already in place in my work with children. However, *Artful–Mindful–Playful* increases the effectiveness of my teaching because for me, it makes the lesson more intentional. I can focus on several "power standards" in our district's curriculum, connecting them through singing, moving, and playing instruments.

 Even though this lesson focused on simple rhythmic concepts, the inclusion of many other musical elements was the serendipitous by-product of engaged, processed, active music making experiences.

Project 2-Davis

Rhythm Project: Grades: 2–3

Half note:

Repertoire: *Listen to the Sun Music For Children*, American Edition, Vol. II, p. 191
Who's That Tapping at the Window? APM, p. 55

Lesson Developer: Leonard Davis

Making Music

Students travel in shared space with feet matching note values played on unpitched percussion

- In personal space and scattered throughout the room, students move their bodies, first in place and then traveling about the room to sound cues given by the teacher. The focus is on movement that matches the beat and movements that are sustained and last longer than one beat (augmented beat).

- *Let's play a movement game! I will play on the temple blocks and your feet will match what you hear. When the sound stops, you must freeze with both feet on the floor! Be careful to listen to the temple block and move according to the sounds you hear.*

Teacher plays quarter note beat (walking) ♩ ♩ ♩ ♩

Teacher plays eighth note subdivided beat ♫ ♫ ♫ ♫

Teacher alternates between playing beat and subdivided beat and pausing, based on students reaction abilities.

What if I played the finger cymbals? How could you move your feet to match the longer sounds?
Teacher plays half notes and students glide/slide around room ♩ ♩

Students recognize longer and shorter sounds in a poem

- *Listen to a poem while you pat the beat.*

Listen to the sun, ♫ ♫ ♩

Listen to the sun, ♫ ♫ ♩

Listen to the sunshine, ♫ ♫ ♩ ♩

All day long. ♩ ♩ ♩

- *Which words in the poem are longer?* (sun and long) *In what ways could we use our bodies to show the longer sounds when we speak the poem?* Examples: hands move up and over the head to create an arch that represents the sun, take one hand and move across the opposite arm.
- *Let's say the poem and show our ways to represent our longer sounds. Now, let's clap on the word "sun-shine." Now, let's pat on "listen to the." Can we put the whole thing together? Can we think the words and perform the movement alone?*

Students learn *Who's That?* and identify half note

Students learn words through echo imitation. Words can be displayed as a visual.

Who's   that   tap-ping at the win- dow? Who's   that   knock-ing at the door?
Ma - ma's   Pa - pa's

- Students speak the words and pat the beat. Students identify the words that are longer (*Who's/that/Ma-ma's/Pa-pa's*). Students find a way to clap the longer sounds (example: clap and then draw hand up other arm for two beats).
- *When we hear a sound lasting for two beats we call it a half note. We can say "ta-ah" for our special rhythm language.*

Making Up Music

Students arrange rhythm motifs based on quarter, eighth, and half notes

- I created the following visuals for students on index cards:

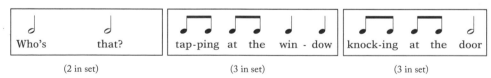

Who's   that?   tap-ping at the win - dow   knock-ing at the door

(2 in set)   (3 in set)   (3 in set)

Each set included eight cards, two containing the two half notes/*Who's that* rhythm, three with tapping at the window/*ti-ti ti-ti ta ta*, and three with knocking at the door/*ti-ti ti-ti* half note). Students worked with partners to create original eight-beat phrases. Students then selected four cards to arrange in order to create their own sixteen-beat compositions. One partner was in charge of keeping a steady beat and the other was in charge of saying the words and clapping the rhythm. If this was done successfully each pair was given unpitched percussion.

One instrument (wood block, claves, rhythm sticks was used for quarter note and eighth notes and the other (finger cymbals, triangle) was used for half notes. My students loved the challenge of creating their "own" piece using words from the poem from the previous week. Many groups had the chance to share with the rest of the class with the remaining lesson time.

Making Sense of Music

Students demonstrate understanding of half note by matching rhythm patterns to speech and aurally discriminating between two rhythm patterns

What do you hear? Circle your answer.

What would this sound like? Draw a line from sentence to the matching rhythm.

1. Ring around the moon

2. Tapping at the window

3. Who's That?

Reflections

This was a first *APM* curricular model for a younger grade. My first application of this model began with the older grades because I have been their music teacher for longer and I knew that they had many and varied experiences in music making and creating that led to conceptual understanding. It has also been my experience that my older age students can reach perceptual awareness of a new rhythm or pitch element because they have the musical foundation to understand thinking in sound. My younger students were going to need more experiences in the Making Music before we could move on to Making Up and Making Sense. Therefore I found this model working best with my younger grades when I spent 2–3 lessons with *APM*.

Previous attempts at teaching half note to younger students have been primarily singing only. I believe strongly that singing is a direct and immediate experience for both pitch and rhythm understanding. I wanted to do things differently by emphasizing more on movement and the body and connecting speech to rhythm—both chief characteristics of the Orff-Schulwerk approach. Singing during these lessons came at the start or end of class if we had a few remaining minutes.

Who's That has long been a favorite of mine when introducing the half note. Frazee also recommends it in *APM* as a focus piece for the half note project, but her example includes the rhythm only. I wondered if I could try to introduce the piece first with just speech and then use the piece again in a future half note project with my students. I am pleased that I did so, because when it came to the Making Up week and creating arrangement using motifs from *Who's That?*, students were focused on speaking the words in rhythm and clapping/playing the note values. The result was that I wasn't concerned about in-tune singing when the song phrases were rearranged.

Many of these ideas for this project were taken directly from studying Frazee's work in *Orff–Schulwerk Today*.[1] In addition to *Artful–Playful–Mindful*, this book has been my bible for resources and objectives for my students when I craft an *APM* project. When first developing this project I went to her section on rhythm and was pleased to find many different ideas for the half note rhythm!

This project is the first of two half note projects that I will develop with my second graders. The second project will come at the end of the year when students have more experience and greater musical skills. That second project will include a greater emphasis on improvisation in the Making Up week and more on notation. This first half note project has been an introduction to the element. My priority outcomes were to help students to recognize sounds that are longer than one beat, to physically feel the duration of words in speech, and that those sounds that last for two beats are half notes. This decision made notation a secondary objective—I only wanted students to recognize what a half note looks like, but not apply it to their own compositions at this point.

Project 3-Larsen

Rhythm Project: ♪♩ ♪ Grades: 4–5

Repertoire: *Alabama Gal, APM*, p. 57

Lesson Developer: Diana Larsen

Making Music

Students perform, aurally analyze and identify the syncopated rhythmic figure ♪♩ ♪

- Students sing and dance "Alabama Gal" in a longways set (as learned from Peter & Mary Alice Amidon).

1. Come through 'na hurry… *Top couple sashays down and back*
2. I don't know how, how… *All right hand turn, then left hand turn partner*
3. I'll show you how, how… *Top couple lead others and cast off to bottom*
4. Ain't I rock candy… *Top couple makes two-handed arch at bottom, other couples take partner's hand below the arch, walk under the arch and back to the top of the set*

- Students sing all verses seated while performing a body percussion ostinato.

- Half of the class maintains BP ostinato, while the other half claps and speaks the text to the "Ain't I rock candy" verse. Switch so all students perform both parts.
- *Does our ostinato match* "Ain't I rock candy?" *What do you notice?* Students determine "I" is longer than "ain't" and "rock."

- Students explore placing ties between different notes:

- Students tie second and third notes together (♪♪♪♪ to ♪ ♩ ♪). We call this "ti-ta-ti" or "syncopa."

Making Up Music
Students compose sixteen-beat rhythm patterns that include ♪ ♩ ♪

- Present and explore U.S. map. Class, I love our state of Iowa, but I have had enough of this long winter. Let's take a trip! Teacher resumes known body percussion ostinato (♫ ♫ ♩ ♩) and speaks *Let's go to Mississippi* (♪♩ ♪♫ ♫). *Who would like to join me?* Then you say, "I'll go to Mississippi." *Where would you like to go?*

- Game in a seated circle, students take turns sharing where they would like to go while maintaining BP ostinato.

  Student: *Let's go to* (state name)
  Class: *I'll go to* (state name)
  Next student: *Let's go to* (state name)
  Class: *I'll go to* (state name), etc.

- Small Group Project Class, you have so many wonderful ideas; now it's time for us to plan some trips. In a few minutes, we will move in to groups of three. Your group will need to decide on three states you would like to visit. Since you will have three people in your group, what would be an easy way to decide which states to include? Right, you each pick one. Or you could consider what one group did in the last class. Aliza just returned from a trip to Indiana. She told me, "Mrs. Larsen, when we drove to Indiana, we went through Illinois twice, once on the way out, and once on the way back." So, her group decided on "Let's go to Illinois, Let's go to Indiana, Let's go to Illinois, Then we'll go home." That's another possibility.

- Students collaborate in small groups to plan their trips, speaking and clapping their piece for the teacher before proceeding to step 3.

  1. Decide where your group would like to travel.

  2. Record the state names in the chart.

♪♩♪		♪♩♪	
Let's go to		Let's go to	
♪♩♪		♪♩♪	♩ 𝄽
Let's go to		Then we'll go	home.

:‖

  3. Perform on instruments. Either 1) all play in unison or 2) take turns.

  Are the instruments your group has chosen good choices for this task?

- Students learn a simple orchestration, which facilitates a class rondo of their ♪♩♪ compositions. The GL/SX part—taught as "pack up and go"—reinforces the syncopated figure, while the BX/BM ostinato requires students to feel the pulse as they shift between half notes and quarter notes layered under syncopation in the other parts.

arranged by Diana Larsen

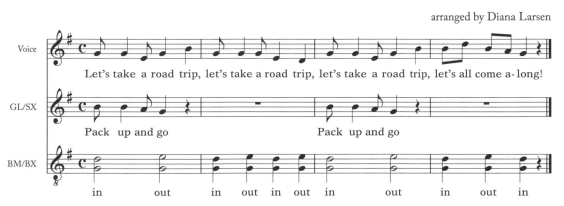

Making Sense of Music

Students demonstrate understanding of ♪ ♩ ♪ by 1) identifying notation that matches the rhythm of a familiar melody, 2) aurally discriminating between two rhythm patterns, and 3) comparing and contrasting ♪ ♩ ♪ and ♩ ♫

1. Our new rhythm pattern looks like this: ♪ ♩ ♪

When we speak it, we can say _____ or _____ .

Think about *Alabama Gal* and the state game we played last week.

2. Which one sounds like *ain't I rock candy?*

a) ♪ ♩ ♪ ♩ ♩

b) ♫ ♫ ♩

c) ♪ ♩ ♪ ♫ ♫

3. Which one sounds like *let's go to Colorado?*

a) ♪ ♩ ♪ ♩ ♩

b) ♫ ♫ ♩

c) ♪ ♩ ♪ ♫ ♫

4. What do you hear?

a) 𝄴 ♫ ♩ ♩ ♩ | ♪ ♩ ♪ ♩ ‡ ‖

b) 𝄴 ♪ ♩ ♪ ♩ ♩ | ♪ ♩ ♪ ♩ ‡ ‖

5. What do you hear?

a) 𝄴 ♩ ♫ ♩ ♩ | ‡ ♩ ♩ ‡ ‖

b) 𝄴 ♪ ♩ ♪ ♩ ♩ | ‡ ♩ ♩ ‡ ‖

How do you know that you can speak, sing, play and read ♪ ♩ ♪ ?

What strategies do you use to help you?

_____

_____

_____

_____

Use the Venn Diagram below to compare and contrast ♪♩ ♪ and ♩ ♫

Record what is different about ♪♩ ♪ and ♩ ♫ in the outer part of each circle. Record what is the same where the circles overlap.

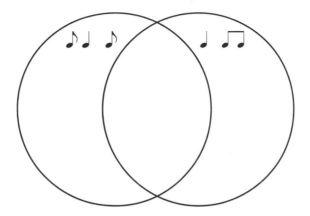

Reflections

While planning this project, my goals included 1) selecting a folk dance with ♪♩ ♪ to open *Artful* week, 2) developing an original game that would lead to a creative task, and 3) experimenting with a Venn Diagram as a tool to develop mindfulness.

On day one I taught my students *Alabama Gal* as I would most folk dances—by keeping teacher talk to a minimum and the kids in motion, learning the tune and lyrics as they go. When the children returned later in the week and were familiar enough with the song to sing it independently and artfully while performing the dance with reasonable accuracy, I added a sparse, chordal accompaniment at the piano, careful not to bury their singing. In the Project Model, I find that when I insist the children take the lead as they make artful music, they draw on these experiences when making up music and making sense of music.

To open *Playful* week, I designed a game that would allow for speech practice with the added challenge of maintaining a non-syncopated body percussion ostinato. I projected a giant map of the United States and set up the game using "I do, we do, you do" instruction. Many students said the names of states they had traveled to, while most of my ELL students showed relief that they had the option to repeat a state someone else had already shared.

In my first attempt at the small group project, I asked students to notate the state rhythms and gave them the option to include the body percussion ostinato in their composition. This was too much for some of the groups, as they became understandably confused by anacrusis in the state names. In between classes, I simplified the task since the aim was not to notate complicated rhythms. I also left out the ostinato option, instead asking the groups to perform in unison or taking turns. This kept them focused on performing ♪♩ ♪ while giving them the choice and flexibility to explore timbre.

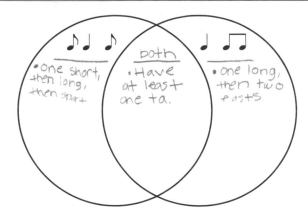

In this assessment, I intended to give my students many different types of tasks to demonstrate understanding. I knew they had used Venn Diagrams in language arts, but I was curious to see how they would respond to one in a music setting. In my own education I had used Venn Diagrams to compare and contrast musical works, but never with something as focused as two-beat rhythmic figures.

Reviewing my students' diagrams helped me get a better grasp of how they think about notation. I was surprised that not one of them suggested that both figures equal two beats in duration. Most wrote about order and each note's individual duration. I wonder if this would have been different had I left the figures in the context of a 2- or 4-beat measure.

While *What do you hear?* questions ask students to apply their understanding, this type of task helps the teacher better to understand how they make sense of the concept as they apply it. Ideally, this feedback will lead to more enlightened instruction down the road.

Project 4-Bergeron

Rhythm Project: 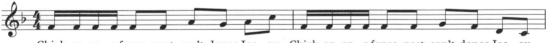 **Grades: 4–5**

Repertoire: *Dance Josey, Discovering Orff,* p. 155
Ding Dong, Diggidiggidong, Music for Children Vol. I, p. 24

Lesson Developer: Rachel Bergeron

Making Music

Students identify and perform rhythm patterns containing the four sixteenth note rhythm figure.

- Teach *Dance Josey* by rote. Walk the beat CCW in a circle while singing the song (this serves as preparation for the game later in class).

Dance Josey

American folk song

Chick-en on a fence-post, can't dance Jos- ey. Chick-en on a fence-post, can't dance Jos- ey.

Chick-en on a fence-post, can't dance Jos - ey. Hel - lo Sus - an Brown.

- Introduce a speech and body percussion ostinato that contains the sixteenth note rhythm figure. Teach the ostinato by rote, clapping the top line and patting the bottom line (see figure below).

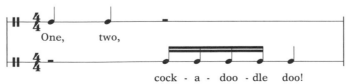

One, two,

cock - a - doo - dle doo!

- Move students into two concentric circles. (This also prepares them for playing the game.) The inside circle performs the ostinato while the outside circle sings. Switch parts.
- Display four beats with the text, "One, two, cock-a-doo-dle-doo," underneath. Guide students to write the rhythms above. Introduce the set of four sixteenth notes. Demonstrate how to write them, four sticks, with 2 beams (just like a fencepost!)

    NOTE: I used a graphic of a fencepost and placed the text inside. (see below). When my students reached the beat above "cock-a-doo-dle," their first solution was to write two pairs of eighth notes. I reminded them that each box could only receive one beat and used guiding questions to help them discover four sixteenth notes as the solution for beat 3.

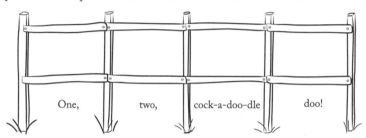

- Display the following visual to show the rhythm sequence. Practice reading each line using rhythm syllables. In my classes, we use *ta* for quarter notes, *ta-di* for eighth notes, and *ta-ka-di-mi* for sixteenth notes.

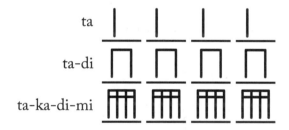

- Display a visual of the rhythm for *Chicken On A Fencepost*. Read rhythm using rhythm syllables.

Dance Josey
Rhythms

Students perform ostinati containing the four sixteenth note rhythm figure as an accompaniment.

- Sing *Ding, Dong, Diggidiggidong.* Ask students to identify the sixteenth notes aurally in the song. Students play the sixteenth note rhythm on their legs whenever they hear it in the song. Teach the song by rote.
- Display the rhythm notation for *Ding, Dong, Diggidiggidong.* Ask students to read rhythms using the *ta-ka-di-mi* system of syllables.

- Students move to barred instruments set up in C pentatonic. Teach students to play the first measure through echo-playing, starting with just quarter notes, then adding the sixteenth note figure. Sing the song, asking students to play measures one and three, while the teacher plays measures two and four. Once students are confident in playing the first measure, select students to play it as an ostinato while the rest of the class sings the song.

Ding, Dong, Diggidiggidong

Orff/Keetman

Ding, dong, dig-gi-dig-gi-dong, dig-gi-dig-gi-dong, the cat she's gone.

Ding, dong, dig-gi-dig-gi-dong, dig-gi-dig-gi-ding dang dong.

- Lead students to discover that the first phrase of *Ding Dong Diggidiggidong* uses the same rhythm as the ostinato for *Dance Josey*. Review the ostinato (one, two, cock-a-doodle doo) and transfer it to temple blocks or barred instruments set in F pentatonic.

    NOTE: I accompanied the song using a broken drone in F pentatonic. Students who played the ostinato on barred instruments explored ways of playing the rhythm in a variety of ways: on just the home note, using both tonic and dominant, and adding additional notes in the pentatonic.

- Play the game: Students hold hands in two concentric circles. Put a rubber chicken or other object representing the "chicken" in the center of the inside circle. Choose two students who will race for the chicken. Select two secret "gates" (students who will drop their hands) that will open at the end of the song. Sing the song while walking, each circle turning in opposite directions. Select students to play the ostinato for an introduction and accompaniment. Teacher or student may choose to accompany the song with broken drone played on the bass xylophone.

- At the end of the song, the "gates" open and the two students race through the gates to get to the center. The first one to pick up the chicken in the middle wins the game. The winner of the game becomes the next student to play the ostinato on the temple blocks.

Making Up Music

Students arrange rhythms containing sixteenth notes to create a rhythmic piece.

- Review *Ding, Dong, Diggidiggidong*. Identify the phrase form of the song (ABAC). Display the following rhythms, text, and body percussion.

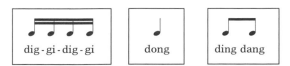

- Play 4-beat rhythmic phrases using body percussion and rhythm syllables for students to echo back.

dig - gi - dig - gi   ding   dang   dig - gi - dig - gi   dong

Examples:

ding   dang   dig - gi - dig - gi   dig - gi - dig - gi   dong

- Display the following six rhythms:

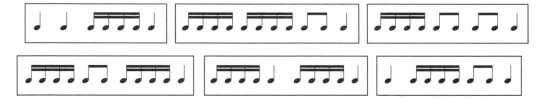

- As a class, practice reading the rhythms using the text and body percussion. Divide students into groups of three. Ask students to arrange phrases to create a 4-measure, 16-beat piece. Three different phrases will be used; one phrase will be repeated.

  Here is the teaching sequence I used:

  ○ Students individually select a rhythm and create a way of playing it using body percussion. They can choose to use the body percussion explored at the beginning of class or create their own.

  ○ Students share their individual rhythms and way of playing with their group.

  ○ Groups create a form for their three rhythms (*abca, abac, aabc, abbc,* etc) and practice playing their rhythm piece together.

  ○ Provide additional time for students to analyze and make changes—add dynamics, add levels or movement, add instruments, explore connecting within their group, or develop speech to match.

  ○ At the end of class, groups perform their rhythms using body percussion, speech, and/or instruments. Perform as a rondo, using the song, *Ding Dong Diggidiggidong* as the A section for the performance.

Making Sense of Music
Rhythm Dictation

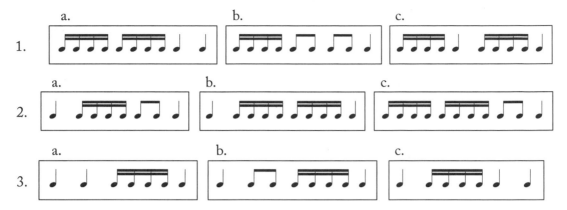

Write the rhythm for the following:

1. *Chicken on the fencepost, can't dance Josey*
2. *Ding, dong, diggi-diggi-dong*

Notation
Sudents perform their rhythm piece from the previous *Playful* lesson. Identify the rhythms they selected for each phrase.

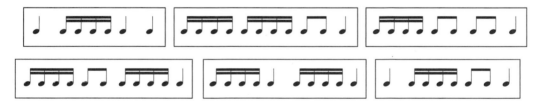

Reflections
This lesson sequence has been slightly condensed and revised from what I initially presented in the classroom. Based on my reflection of the lessons and on how my students responded, I have chosen to focus the lessons around just two song selections: *Dance Josey*, an American folk-song, and *Ding, Dong, Diggidiggidong*, a well-known canon from Volume I of *Music for Children*.

Artful
One of the things that first drew me to the *APM* model was that it encourages the teacher to find the musical examples that: 1) are interesting, 2) are memorable, and 3) invite further encounters (*Artful–Playful–Mindful*, p. 10). These two songs fit this model: they serve as good pedagogical models for introducing and exploring sixteenth notes, are engaging for the students, and allow students to delve more deeply into the material.

I chose *Dance Josey* because of its repetitive rhythmic form and appeal to students, and included *Ding Dong Diggidiggidong* because it works well as a model for composition. *Dance*

Josey is one of my students' favorite singing games, so one of my goals was finding a way to include the game in the lesson while still keeping the focus on sixteenth notes.

One of the things I considered while planning these lessons was the development of technical skills needed to play the faster sixteenth notes, particularly on barred instruments. In this unit, I initially explored the use of floor drums (congas or tubanos) as a way of experiencing 16th rhythms. However, in the end, I realized patting sixteenth notes on the body and playing simple ostinato accompaniments—both using alternating hands—was simpler and more effective.

Playful

In *Artful–Playful–Mindful*, Frazee describes the active musical exploration in the O–S classroom as "using playful means to achieve musical ends" (p. 18). Through playful exploration in collaboration with others, students created rhythm pieces. This task of composing allowed them to function as musicians—expressing their musical ideas, analyzing and revising them throughout the process, and eventually finding ways to remember them through notation.

The *Playful* rhythm project grew out of my desire to have students compose with sixteenth notes, but provide enough structure that they could be successful within a 30-minute class. I included rhythms from our work so some would be familiar. I also provided a structure for developing the piece and establishing the form so students would have time to develop and perform a four-measure piece.

The sequence I used for the rhythm project is something I have used in a variety of areas, such as creating melodies, sequencing movement, and composing with rhythms. It works off the basic Orff principal of simple-to-complex. Each student begins with a simple idea, which then must be taught to other individuals. Through the process of creating and then teaching it, the rhythm or phrase is internalized and the material is more easily remembered. Through collaboration, the simple idea is developed into something much more complex. It also challenges each student to play an active role in the collaboration.

My role during most of the lesson was to move around the room, listening to students work, asking questions, and making suggestions as needed. I offered those groups who were working quickly toward their finished product the opportunity to add instruments, movement, or speech to their creations. Some groups needed to add levels or movement, or connect with their group members to make their performance piece more visually interesting. Others needed guidance in understanding the form and making sure their rhythms and body percussion were accurate.

Mindful

During performances, when groups are working with assigned rhythms, I often ask the audience to identify the rhythms used by the performers. It is a good assessment tool, and gives the listener a specific task to focus on during the performance. I didn't do this during the *Playful* section because I didn't want to take time away from developing and performing the rhythms. However, I realized by recording student performances that I could use the same questioning process for assessment during the *Mindful* lesson.

The use of technology for reflecting and assessing is a great tool! Students were excited to watch recorded performances of themselves and their classmates. This was an effective way of assessing and reviewing the material performed in the previous class.

Project 5-Davis

Rhythm Project: ♫♫ **Grades: 6–7**

Repertoire: *Old Betty Larkin*, folk song

Bubblegum, Bubblegum traditional chant with adaptation

Musette in D J.S. Bach

Lesson Developer: Leonard Davis

Making Music
Students identify and perform rhythm patterns containing two 16th-8th note rhythm figures.

- Students sing and play *Old Betty Larkin*

Hop a-round, skip a-round Old Bet-ty Lar-kin, Hop a-round, skip a-round Old Bet-ty Lar-kin,

Hop a-round, skip a-round, Old Bet-ty Lark-kin, Al - so my dear dar - ling.

2. Needle in a haystack, Old Betty Larkin, (3x)
   Also, my dear darling.
3. Steal, steal, Old Betty Larkin, (3x)
   Also, my dear darling
4. You'll take mine, I'll take another, (3x)
   Also, my dear darling

- Game: Students start by standing in a circle formation and holding hands with a partner. An extra person stands in the center of the circle. During verse 1, the student in the inside of the circle skips clockwise around the inside of the circle while the students in the circle join hands with their partner and skip around counterclockwise. During verse 2, the students stop skipping and face in towards the middle of the circle while the extra student skips around the circle and takes a partner. Those two students then skip around the circle until they arrive back to where the partner was taken. During this time, the student whose partner was taken quickly takes a different partner, and so on. This continues for verses 3 and 4. At the end of verse 4, the movement stops and the student without a partner is the extra player in the circle and is ready for the dance to continue again. The game generates a lot of excitement—my students loved the stealing aspect of this game!

- Teacher leads students to discover the two 16th-8th figure through a series of questions:

Teacher and students sing the first phrase of *Old Betty Larkin*.

How many beats are in the first phrase? (4)

How many sounds are on beat one? (3)

Are they even or uneven? (uneven)

What is the pattern of long and short sounds? (short-short-long)

Hop a-round, skip a-round Old Bet-ty Lark-kin.

- Teacher notates the first phrase of *Old Betty Larkin*. Students read rhythm pattern containing two 16th-8th note figure. They are able to read the third beat, one 8th-two 16th note figure from a previous rhythm project.

- Students read four-beat rhythm patterns containing focus rhythm from visuals. Possibilities:

Making Up Music

Students improvise 8-beat rhythm patterns containing two 16th 8th note rhythm figure.

- "Let's move our bodies around the room and carry the beat in our feet! When the sound stops, freeze with your feet on the floor!" Teacher plays the beat/pulse on the temple blocks and students travel and explore space around the room. Teacher changes from beat to subdivided beat and then to rhythm patterns containing two 16th 8th notes.

- "Now I am going to chant a poem and play the rhythm on the temple block. You can echo back and move your feet to the rhythm!"

Bubblegum, Bubblegum, in a dish,

How many pieces do you wish?

One o'clock, two o'clock, three o'clock, four,

Take a piece of candy and have some more!

- Students chant *Bubblegum* poem and clap rhythm from visual. Students identify beats containing focus rhythm.
- Students read rhythms from visuals associated with different types of sweet foods/candy.

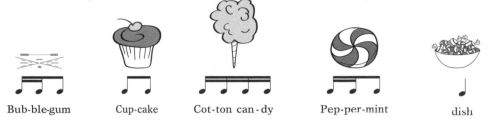

| Bub-ble-gum | Cup-cake | Cot-ton can-dy | Pep-per-mint | dish |

- "Let's create an eight beat rhythm pattern containing our candy rhythms." Students create and clap as a class an eight beat rhythm. Example:

- "Let's read and clap our pattern again, but when we get to a question mark, you can decide what rhythm you want to use. When we create on the spot, remember that we call that improvising!"

1)

2)

3)

4)

- Students begin by improvising for two beats only (figure 1). Once comfortable, students can work towards improvising for seven beats (figures 2 and 3) and end together with a quarter note (figure 4). Student improvisations can serve as the interludes sections between *Bubblegum* poem. My students were able to improvise with confidence in small groups and independently and were able to play their improvisations on unpitched percussion.

Making Sense of Music

Students notate an 8-beat rhythm patterns containing two 16th-8th note rhythm figure.

- "Last week we improvised using our new rhythm. Today let's take that rhythm and compose a pattern. We will practice notating our rhythms."
- Student examples:

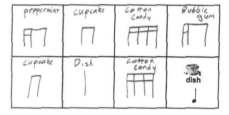 

Students identify two 16th-8th note rhythm figure in Bach's *Musette in D*

Bach's *Musette in D* is a short example with clear use of the two 16th-8th note figure. Students can identify the focus rhythm from a visual of the piece and can read the rhythm of the entire A section before the teacher plays the example at the piano or a recording of this well-known piece.

Musette in D

J.S. Bach

Student Reflection

Students are given the opportunity to reflect upon their learning by answering questions related to their rhythmic understanding. Questions can be answered on the back of their composition assignment. Examples:

1. How do you know that you can read, write, and perform patterns with two 16th-8th note?

2. What strategies do you use to help you?

Reflection

I selected *Old Betty Larkin* as one of the pieces for this project because of my fondness for the American Play Party repertoire and the power that these songs and dances have over my students. The magic of the Play Parties is confirmed by the smiles and laughter of my students and the unanimous "Can we do it again?" from the class. As part of the America folk culture from long ago, these pieces are a wonderful source of song material for elementary aged children. I encourage the reader to find *Waltz the Hall: The American Play Party* [1] by Alan Spurgeon if they would like more information and are looking for a repertoire resource.

Old Betty Larkin is a very clear example of the rhythm element two 16th-8th note on the first two beats of the first phrase of the song, and because of the repetition of playing the game, my students were able to reach the perceptual understanding (three uneven sounds on a beat with the pattern short-short-long) very quickly. Because they had also encountered the element in reverse (8th-16th) earlier in the year, they were able to see and hear the difference and read patterns with fluency.

For our playful event, I chose the *Bubblegum* chant with a personal adaptation because it also featured the pattern on the first two beats of the first phrase, just like *Old Betty Larkin*. This experience began with movement and connecting the rhythmic speech to patterns in our feet. I also knew that I could create an improvisation experience based on the element and by using words from the poem and other candy names because my students have had very similar experiences in the past with rhythm improvisation based on words and themes (names, colors, fruits, state capitols, etc.) The highlight of the Making Music lesson was when students were able to improvise alone and put the words "inside" their heads. Using the poem as the A section and the student improvisations at the interludes, the students wanted to improvise alone and in duets for the whole class. This was a rewarding experience for both them and their teacher.

For Making Sense week, I chose to have the students take their ideas from the Making Up week and notate patterns using the two 16th-8th note rhythm figure. Students were able to notate a pattern that they had created from the previous week's lesson, or come up with one very quickly. Finally, we used a well-known Bach piece that also highlighted the rhythm element. I began by playing the A section of the piece to see if students could aurally identify the rhythm pattern, and to my delight they were able both to hear and find it! We were then able to find the notation in the piece and could clap rhythm patterns from the *Musette*. When I repeat this project again in the future I want also to include the opportunity for students to dictate patterns that I play for them so that I can see they are able to hear and then notate what they have heard.

Project 6-Larsen

Rhythm Project: ♪. ♪ **Grades: 6–7**

Repertoire: *Bats Eat Bananas* (Khaang Khaaw Kin Kluay), Thai Traditional

Lesson Developer: Diana Larsen

Introduction

From 2004–2009 I taught elementary music at International School Bangkok, a private PreK-12 school that serves that expatriate community of Bangkok, Thailand. In addition to learning from talented colleagues who had more experience with the Orff Approach than I did at the time, I became close with Khun Patty, the instructional assistant who supported the music department. Showing incredible patience, Khun Patty taught me several Thai songs and games, carefully coaching me on pronunciation and style. At some point in our collaboration, we came to *Khaang Khaaw Kin Kluay* (Bats Eat Bananas), which coincidentally aligned with the week my husband and I were learning the names of fruits and vegetables in our Thai lessons. For some reason, the piece captured my imagination, and I knew my older students would love the challenge of performing the playful melody on xylophones.

Over time I experimented with ways to adapt the piece for use with children without compromising the integrity or the authenticity of the piece, but it wasn't until years later—when I was taking an Orff Curriculum Development course with Jay Broeker—that I settled on an approach that I felt would be successful and purposeful with students. One of the assignments was to plan and teach a sequence of lessons that developed one musical concept over two days. I examined the melody, and the opening dotted 8th 16th figure jumped off the page. I will focus on the rhythm concept of ♪. ♪ After listening to several versions of the Thai traditional on YouTube, I decided to focus on the A section, which is in abab' form. Elemental form—yes! Then I remembered a lesson I learned from Jo Ella Hug that pulled in Keith Terry's body percussion technique. Maybe there's a way for my students to move and feel the subdivisions before moving in to the new rhythm figure. The ideas were coming together, but I wondered how effectively I could focus on a concept without losing the piece's cultural essence, its Thainess. I decided to provide some context by setting up the musical instruction with a brief geography lesson followed by a story inspired by an image of the Thai country-side at dusk. I also planned to incorporate a *ching*, Thai finger cymbals, into the arrangement.

A year or two later, after I had taught the arrangement to several groups of students, Leonard Davis encouraged me to take another look at this series of lessons to determine how they might work within the project model. Were there artful, playful and mindful components? I felt I could safely answer yes to the first two criteria, but I had not yet written assessable outcomes that would drive mindful conversations and tasks. When working with children on this piece, I had gotten so wrapped up in the performance aspect—fine arts night was just around the corner—that I found myself in the habit of ending the process prematurely. I had taken my kids all the way around the block, but stopped short of bringing them home. What could they really tell me about what they had performed?

So, as I took another look at my lesson design and teaching process, I determined what I really wanted my students to understand, know and do: They should know how ♩. ♪ *Ta-mi/* dotted 8th 16th figure relates to the pulse and other notes. They should be able to analyze an excerpt with ♩. ♪ , matching what they hear with what they see as music notation. And through their work with an artful piece from another part of the world, they begin to build understanding of how music and culture relate to one another.

Making Music
Students perform ♩. ♪ as body percussion, with text, and on barred instruments.

Preparation
- Begin class non-verbally with 4-beat echo imitation using traditional body percussion levels (stamp, pat, clap and snap). Perform the beat as a stamp and ♫♫ as pats.
- Once the pulse and subdivisions have been established, introduce 1 2 3 4 5 (♫♫♪) as clap chest chest pat pat (in the style of Keith Terry) into the body percussion. At first, speak all of the numbers while playing the body, then just 1 4 5, and eventually just sound 1 4 5 as body percussion.
- In other words, ♩. ♪ ♩ sounds as clap ✓✓ pat pat.

Context
- Display a world map (figure 1) showing Thailand relative to home. Today we're going to take a trip to the other side of the world. Does anyone know which country this is? What is the climate in Thailand? How do you know it's tropical? Right, it's close to the equator. Seeing that tropical Thailand is on the other side of the world—12 hours ahead of us, actually—do you think we would see the same kinds of plants and animals living there as we do in the temperate Midwest? Which reminds me of the time…

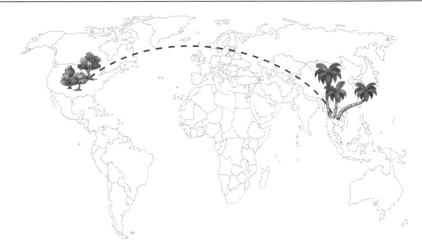

Figure 1

- Story: Once, while on an evening walk in Thailand (figure 2), I noticed mysterious shapes in the sky swooping into the banana groves followed by an eerie stillness. At first I thought they were birds, but after taking a closer look I noticed they were definitely not birds. What were they? Yes, bats! And these bats were different than the bats I had seen growing up in the Midwest because they don't just eat mosquitos; they eat fruit! And these bats enjoyed a feast of bananas that warm evening in Thailand.

Figure 2

- Perform speech piece in its entirety, then teach it to class through echo imitation. At this stage, the students refer to the text without notation.

a	b	a	b'
Fly then perch Fly then perch	munching, munching fruits of Thailand—yes, they do!	Fly then perch Fly then perch	munching, munching lots of fruit!

Fly, then perch, fly, then perch, munch-ing, munch-ing fruits of Thai-land, yes they do!

Fly, then perch, fly, then perch, munch-ing, munch-ing lots of fruit!

- Add movement: (a) leap, step, step; repeat (b) change direction; (b') arrive at starting point by final word "fruit."
- Then perform body percussion as students listen for 1 4 5 from opening. Students join during the a sections, then b and b' as they become familiar with the patterns.

cl p p   cl p p   p p p p cl cl   cl cl sn sn sn   cl p p   cl p p   p p p p cl cl   st

- Students set up barred instruments in F pentatonic while the teacher plays the xylophone melody on a recorder. Listening to two measures at a time, students find the melody on their xylophones. I recommend starting with measures 1–2 and 5–6, then adding measures 7–8, and finally filling the gap with measures 3–4.
- Add bordun and finger cymbals. To emulate the *ching*, or Thai finger cymbals, alternate a sustained "ching" with a dampened "chop."

- Before moving to the next step, students move away from the instruments and gather at the SmartBoard.

  Students identify and label the rhythmic figure ♩. ♪ as "Ta mi."

> Learn more about the Takadimi system for developing rhythm skills in *Takadimi: A Beat-Oriented System of Rhythm Pedagogy* by Richard Hoffman, William Pelto, and John W. White as printed in the *Journal of Music Theory Pedagogy*, Vol. 10 (1996) 7–30.
>
>
>
> Ta   Ta-di   Ta-ka-di-mi   Ta-ka-di   Ta-di-mi

- Echo imitate familiar rhythm patterns *t, td, tkdm, tkd* and *tdm.*

  1. as speech
  2. as body percussion

        t = clap

        t d = clap, chest

        t k d = clap, chest, chest

        t k d m = clap, chest, chest, pat

        t d m = clap, chest, pat

  3. as speech and body percussion

Examples:

Teacher						Students							
t		t		t		t	t		t		t		t
t		t	d	t	d	t	t		t	d	t		t
t	k	d	t	k	d	t		t	k	d	t	k	d	t		t
t	k	d	m	t		t	k	d	m	t	t	k	d	m	t		t	K	d	m	t
t		T		t	d	m	t	t		t		t	d	m	t

- Students read and perform familiar rhythms from "duration notation."

1. | Ta-ka-di-mi | Ta | Ta-ka-di-mi | Ta |

2. | Ta-di | Ta-ka-di-mi | Ta | Ta-di |

3. | Ta-ka-di | Ta-ka-di | Ta-di | Ta |

4. | Ta-ka-di-mi | Ta-di | Ta-ka-di | Ta |

5. | Ta-ka-di | ⅔ | Ta-ka-di | Ta |

- Students match text with duration notation, dragging and dropping duration notion choices, and identify "fly, then perch" as something else.

Thailand–yes, they do!		
munching, munching fruits of	something else
fruit!		
Fly then perch		⅔

↓

Thailand–yes, they do!		
munching, munching fruits of		
fruit!		⅔
Fly then perch	something else

- Students describe the new rhythm figure in relation to the beat and known patterns, and connect spoken rhythm *Ta-mi ta* to 𝄾

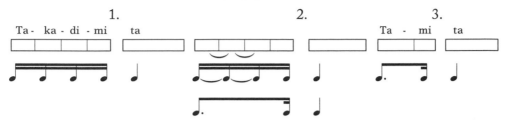

Making Up Music

Students improvise and compose 8-beat phrases using known rhythmic figures and 𝄾

- Students select a rhythmic building block—the same one repeated three times—for the first six beats and end with 𝄾

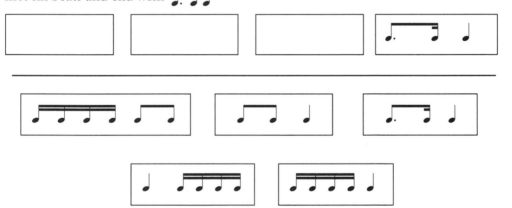

- Students try several possibilities as speech/body percussion, and then select one as a class to explore on barred instruments.

- Students explore the class-composed rhythm on barred instruments in F pentatonic. Process:
  - Play the rhythm
    - on the floor with mallets (reinforce alternating hands)
    - on one bar
    - first three boxes on any one bar, then 𝄾 must be on home tone (F)
  - Students work individually with fingertips to find a good fit for 𝄾 (*ddd, mrd, smd, s,l,d* etc.). Each student selects a favorite version to stick with throughout the following steps, the key being that he or she can play it with rhythmic accuracy.
  - Teacher guides students to explore melodic shapes for the first six beats:

- Play each of the first three boxes on a different bar, like F, G and A
- Play each ♩♩♩♩♩ on two bars, then three. Could you play ♩♩♩♩♩ on four or five bars? What makes that challenging?
- Settle on one way to perform the class-composed rhythm as a melody. We should hear ♩♩♩♩♩ three times followed by one ♩. ♩ ♩
  - Students practice independently for a few minutes (either with fingertips or quiet mallets) to transition their explorations to composition.
  - After a group practice, students play their melodies for a nearby classmate.
- TASK: Now that each of you has composed your own melody from our class-composed rhythm and performed it for a classmate, I'd like you to develop a plan with this partner. You may:
  1. Play your melodies at the same time, or
  2. Bring your ideas together to create a new melody.
  - If you would like, you may select a new rhythm for the first three boxes, but you must end with ♩. ♩ ♩ Whatever you decide, we will be listening for three repeated two-beat patterns followed by ♩. ♩ ♩, so make sure you can play your piece accurately! Be ready to share with the class in five minutes.

- This is the time I would typically ask the students to determine a form for a class performance. But because the purpose of this project is to work with ♩. ♩ ♩ as a musician does, we add a step to check for understanding. Each pair performs their composition as the class listens and analyzes what they hear. What did they play? Which rhythm boxes did they use? Did we hear ♩. ♩ ♩ ? When? Did they perform the rhythm accurately? How do you know?

Making Sense of Music

Students demonstrate understanding of ♩. ♩ by 1) aurally discriminating between two rhythm patterns and 2) completing the rhythm notation to a familiar speech piece.

What do you hear? Circle your answer.

3. Complete the missing rhythm notation.

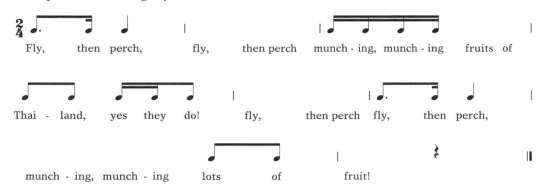

4. A new student named Rebecca joined our class today. At Rebecca's old school, she learned about quarter, eighth and sixteenth notes, but ♩. ♪ is new to her. Using words or pictures, how would you explain what ♩. ♪ is and how it relates to other note values?

5. Why do musicians use music notation? Why is (or isn't) it important?

Reflections

Perhaps the most significant insight I gained from this project was that most of my work was already done. I was already process teaching appropriate, artful materials and guiding my students through playful improvisation and composition tasks, which typically led to pleasing in- and out-of-class performances. So, now I focus my time and energy on expanding the most effective, concept-driven lessons that I already use into *APM* projects that include more significant listening and analysis work, two tasks that are characteristically mindful. I think Frazee specifically sets aside a third of instructional time for mindful tasks because they are the ones so easily overlooked. Our students need this essential piece to truly understand.

In *APM*, Frazee offers dozens of sample mindful activities, many of which are very straightforward and take only a few minutes. While I hope to diversify my approach in time, the most meaningful making sense of music activities I have tried with children have included some sort of pencil-and-paper task with a variety of question types. Can they match what they hear with its corresponding notation? More specifically, can they examine notation and anticipate where in the excerpt they will need to listen for a specific figure? Also, can they analyze and interpret the score of a familiar piece well enough to complete the missing sections, using strategies like checking the time signature, looking for patterns, and most obviously, aligning rhythm notation with text? I have also started including more open-ended questions that ask students to explain their thinking.

> And while [the students are] are thinking and explaining,
> they are demonstrating the learning essentials that we
> have articulated throughout this book: they concentrate,
> analyze and reflect on the musical experiences that have
> led from performing to exploring and ultimately to understanding.

Artful–Playful–Mindful

Part 2: Pitch Projects

Music is the melody whose text is the world

—Arthur Schopenhauer

Project 7-Benson and Smith

Pitch Project: *m-r-d* Grades: 2–3

Repertoire: *#12 Erstes Spiel am Xylophon*, Gunild Keetman

Hot Spicy Tacos (*Hot Cross Buns*) variation adapted by Karen Benson

Carillon from *L' Arlésienne Suite No. 1* Georges Bizet

Lesson Developers: Karen Benson and Shelly Smith

Making Music

Students use movement to learn *#12 Erstes Spiel am Xylophon*

Warm up: Students stand in shared space throughout the room. As the teacher plays one tone on the temple blocks, students are asked to make their feet match the rhythm being played. (Walking = quarter note value.) Using a different pitch, ask students to demonstrate a different rhythm. (Jogging = eighth note value.) Without warning, change the rhythm to see how well they are listening. Ask one group of students to follow the walking rhythm while the other group following the running rhythm. Change parts.

Erstes Spiel am Xylophon

Students echo the following text. Then pat text rhythms, and finally move according to the text directions.

A:

Jogging	Jogging	Jogging	Jogging	Walk	Walk	Stop!	(wait)

B:

Walk	Walk	Stop!	(wait)	Jogging	Jogging	Stop!	(wait)

The form is A A B A

- After students have internalized the melody through movement, move to the barred instruments. Begin by taking off the F and B bars. Ask children to use "finger mallets" to practice the following patterns. As children are able, patterns can be combined until the entire melody is learned.

- At the conclusion of this activity, ask students to identify the number of times and the different ways in which *m-r-d* occurs in this melody.

Making Up Music

Students identify, sing, play and improvise melodic patterns with an emphasis on *m-r-d*

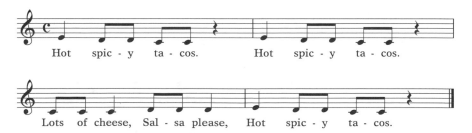

Learn the text through speech and then sing the melody. Next transfer the melody to xylophones having the children sing while they play.

Let students then create ideas for favorite taco toppings using simple or duple rhythm patterns. List and notate the ideas so they are visible to the students.

Students then select and improvise a melodic pattern using only *m-r-d* pitches for their 2-beat taco toppings phrase.

Examples:

| av-o-ca-do | hot pep-pers | ched-dar cheese | corn | pi-co |

Students now play their pattern and have other students guess the topping.

Making Sense of Music

Students demonstrate understanding and application of the *m-r-d* concept through a game setting and listening activity

The game:

Review *Hot Spicy Tacos*. As the song is sung, two students travel around those who are seated on the floor. At the end of the song, they "land" by touching the shoulder of another student. The student who is chosen may:

1. Listen to the teacher sing one of the patterns on solfege syllables. If they correctly identify the pattern, they become the new leader. (Beginning)
2. Listen to the teacher sing one of the patterns on a neutral syllable. (Intermediate)
3. Sing one of the patterns on solfege syllables for another student to identify. (Advanced)

Listening Activity: *Carillon* from *L'Arlésienne Suite No. 1* by Georges Bizet

The challenge of isolating and studying *m-r-d* will be enhanced with the use of a beautiful piece of classical literature and a playful movement activity. In the first 90 seconds of *Carillon*, a repeated *m-d-r* pattern is played by the french horns, written to represent the pealing of church bells.

Introduce the pattern using body solfege to reinforce the pitches.

| *mi* | *do* | *re* |
| Hands on shoulders | Fists at hips | Arms crossed over chest |

Ask students to quietly sing (and sign) the repeated pattern while the music is playing. Add the challenge of students creating different non-locomotor movements or actions to represent the *m-r-d* ostinato.

Reflections

Introducing a melody using locomotor words and movement in the *Artful* section served two purposes. It gave a restless group of 3rd graders an opportunity to get some of the wiggles out early in the lesson while reinforcing rhythms that would ultimately be used in the piece. We work with a fair number of children who are not native English speakers and/or learners with exceptionalities. There are times when using speech alone to reinforce rhythm is challenging for some children. Using speech and movement at the same time helped the children be successful! In addition, students quickly identified the *m-r-d* patterns.

Updating the traditional *Hot Cross Buns* to a topic more relevant to our students gave this useful tune new life in our classrooms. Providing ample, yet informal opportunities to hear, play, and create with the *m-r-d* melodic pattern, prepared the basis of understanding for the students in the *Playful* section of this lesson. The fun of creating the toppings list, followed by the guessing game, engaged the children beyond our expectations. In fact, this game idea became a favorite student request during other creating lessons throughout the school year. The *Hot Spicy Tacos* melody and rhythms also prepared the learners for the *Mindful* stage of the lesson

Finding a way to quickly assess what students know and can demonstrate is an ongoing endeavor. We like to approach this challenge by using some type of "game" to capture the children's interest. Differentiating the assessment based on the comfort level of the student is important for the children we work with. That was also the case with the listening activity. After demonstrating the body solfege and practicing it at tempo we were surprised by the fact most children wanted to perform the more challenging pattern!

In our experience, taking time to discuss the focus of the lesson during several different classes helps the children understand the concept on a much deeper level rather than simply performing the material. *APM* has provided the framework for this type of deeper learning.

Project 8-Larsen

Pitch Project: *d-r-m-s* Grades: 2–3

Repertoire: *Spielstucke #8 Discovering Keetman*, p. 11
Lesson Developer: Diana Hawley Larsen

Making Music

Students sing and play *Take a Walk Now* **(***Spielstucke* **#8), joining known pitch sets** *sm* **and** *mrd*

- Students brainstorm and explore locomotor movements such as walking, running, jumping, tiptoe and skipping while teacher supports with drumming.

Ways to move through space

- walk
- running
- jump
- tiptoe
- skipping

- After removing all F, A and B bars,
  students try out the same movements with their fingertips on barred instruments, freely
  exploring the *smrd* pitch set.

- As I share something new, listen and think about which type of locomotor movement
  would be a good fit for this new melody. Teacher sings melody on "loo." I'm glad you said
  "walking" because the lyrics are: Take a walk now, take a walk now, take a walk now,
  then go home.

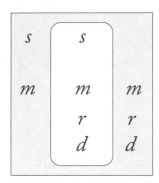

- Today we bring together two sets of pitches—*mrd* and *sm*—into a new piece. What do you notice about this melody? Where does our melody begin? Where does it end? Eventually students decide on *d r m s, d r m s, d r m s, m r d*. Sing with solfege and hand signs.

- What does this melody sound like on your barred instrument? Let's divide our class into two groups of sounds. How should we sort ourselves? (high/low; woods/metals; solo/tutti, etc.) Who should go first? How many times should we play the melody? How many places on your instrument can you play the melody? Play it the first time in one place, and the second time someplace else. Now let's all play it twice on our instruments, first on the longer, lower-pitched bars and second on the shorter, higher-pitched bars.

- What is the shape or contour of this melody? Do the notes move upward or downward? Drag and drop contoured note groupings into place.

- What would this melody look like on the staff?

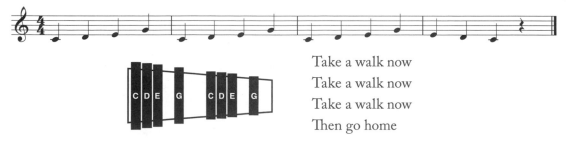

Take a walk now
Take a walk now
Take a walk now
Then go home

Making Up Music
Students compose variations on a known *drms* melody

1. Class, you have shown me that you know a lot about our walking song. You can play it in low and high registers; You can play it on instruments with different timbres or tone colors; You can sing it using *so mi re do*; You have practiced reading it as music notation. Now it's time to play with this melody to create something new!

2. First, let's explore together some ways we could turn the walking song into something new. Remember how we moved last week? What would our walking song sound like as a tiptoe song? Skipping song? Running song? Jumping song? Volunteers demonstrate on a xylophone.

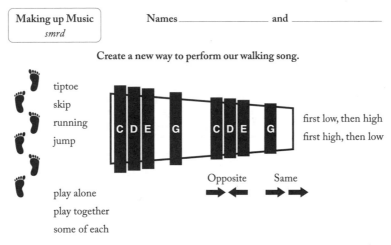

Make up Music / *smrd* — Create a new way to perform our walking song.

Record your ideas here. You may use words or pictures.

3. Since you will be working with a partner, you could also explore taking turns or playing together. What would that sound like?

4. What could first low, then high mean? Maybe one partner plays your idea in the longer bars—in the low register—and then the other plays it on the shorter bars, in the high register. Who can show me what that would look like? What about first high, then low?

5. What could opposite or same mean? Yes, this is about direction! What would it sound like if one partner started on C and played upwards and the other started on G and played downwards?

6. Now you and your partner can get to work! Use an idea we tried as a class to get you started; then try something new. Remember: we want our new pieces to take up the same amount of time as "Take a walk now, take a walk now, take a walk now, then go home." Before you write anything on the paper—notice you can write down your ideas in words, as a drawing or on the music staff—make sure you and your partner can play the piece together.

- In my classroom, this *playful* task took three 25-minute periods to complete.
  - First period—I explained the project, as described above, and partnered the students.

- ○ Second period—I quickly reviewed the task, then let them get to work. I offered support only to pairs who were not playing or talking after several minutes. This is Orff Schulwerk; we have to let them do the work, and that takes time.
- ○ Third period—Students reviewed their work with their partners for a few minutes before I recorded each group's variation with my iPhone for later analysis.

Provided with a "match" and "not a match," students analyze the performances of their classmates, paying attention to contour, register and how the melodies relate to the original.

- Students analyze the full notation of the original piece. We know all about the first line, but what's happening in the second line? Right, it's the same melody starting on the smaller C bar. Even if we aren't used to looking at notes that high on the staff, what can we tell by looking at the shape of the line?

#8 Spielstucke

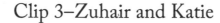

Example 1. Looking at our choices A and B, what would we hear and see if Zuhair and Katie play A? B? What's different about these choices? Yes, B looks like a long line from low to high. Right, A could be the two of them playing at the same time, and B could be them taking turns.

Clip 3–Zuhair and Katie

Example 2. What do you notice about these choices? Right, in A they start close together, moving in opposite directions. In B they move in the same direction.

Clip 4–David and Isaiah

Example 3. An exceptional second grade student, Joanne chose to work by herself after returning from a trip and joining her class mid-project. What will we hear and see if Joanne plays A? Yes, we'd see hands together because the notes are directly above and below each other. What will we see if she plays B? Right, hands taking turns. The students noticed that one of her hands played the same bar the whole time. What does that look like on the staff?

Clip 1–Joanne

Making Sense of Music

Students demonstrate understanding of *drms* by 1) aurally discriminating between two pitch patterns and 2) matching solfege and staff notation.

Name _____

What do you hear? Circle your answer.

What do you see? Draw a line between the matching melodies.

s m r d

s m s m

d r m s

d d m s

- How did you change *Walking Song* to create a new piece?
- What stayed the same? What changed?
- How did you and your partner remember your melody?

Reflections

In *Artful, Playful, Mindful*, Jane Frazee suggests: "reduce the amount of material in order to better exploit its potential for developing musicianship" (p. 1). With this in mind, I set out to find the ideal *drms* piece for my second graders. As I surveyed materials, I kept returning to *Spielstucke #8*. A lovely example of elemental music, the melody ascends through the pitch set three times, eventually walking back to *do*. Beautifully simple, I could see endless possibilities in this piece. All I had to do was figure out how to bring it to life for my kids.

The process I share in this series of lessons has been revised to reflect my own learning from my first attempt at this project. Initially I saved identifying and labeling *drms* until the beginning of Mindful week, thinking that too much direct instruction early in the project might intrude on the playfulness of week two. Yet on reflection I realized the students had ample opportunity to explore the material during the Artful phase and that some students might have made more meaning of their Playful work with the modified sequence I present here.

Create a new way to perform our walking song.

tiptoe
skip
running
jump

C D E G C D E G

first low, then high
first high, then low

play alone
play together
some of each

Opposite   Same

Record your ideas here. You may use words or pictures.

In setting up *Playful* week, I projected this image on the music room SmartBoard and asked my students what they thought I meant by *Create* a new way to perform our walking song. They decided their job was to change something about the piece while keeping some part of it the same. That sounded like a solid second grade definition of a variation to me! One student noticed right away that each xylophone had two sets of *smrd*, and the students realized what taking turns or playing together might look like. Many children were intrigued by the idea of moving in opposite directions, thankful they had permission to make such a significant change to the original melody. I had hoped that the movement preparation at the beginning of the project would have encouraged dynamic (tiptoe) or metric (skip) variation, but most of my students seemed especially eager to modify the rhythm, changing the walking quarters to eighth notes (running).

I use the video camera feature of my phone to record student work or performances in my classroom regularly, but this was the first time I utilized *students' creative work as the musical content of a subsequent lesson.* The kids were thrilled. Shortly into my process of transcribing their variations, I realized I would have to insert a mini lesson on what *drms* looks like an octave higher on the staff. I worried this might move us away from our concept, so I tried to frame that piece of the lesson as a quick extension about contour while always relating the pitches in the higher octave to those in the known register.

Since I built analysis and reflection into my questioning while the students viewed the video clips, I decided on a clear-cut skills assessment with a handful of aural discrimination and matching (solfege to staff notation) questions. I realize at first glance the first questions may look a lot like the kind of testing we're trying to avoid, but in class these analysis tasks come to life. Before asking my seven- and eight-year-olds to do this independently, we do the work as a group at the SmartBoard. *Look at number one. I'm going to play one of these melodies on my recorder, and your job is to figure out which one you hear. What's the difference between the two choices? Right, one of them goes all the way down to* do, *while the other goes up at the end. Everybody know what to listen for? OK—let's try it!*

In terms of student motivation and engagement, this project surpassed my expectations. My second graders still talk about their walking song variations, ask to play them from time to time, and in general, show an eagerness for reworking what they know into something new. In my book, this project was a success.

Project 9-Bergeron

Melody Project: *drm sl d'*   **Grades: 4–5**

Repertoire: *Tideo* folk song
Diddle Diddle Dumply poem, *Exploring Orff*, p. 164
Canon #4, Music For Children, Vol. I, p. 91

Lesson Developer: Rachel Bergeron

Making Music

Students sing, read, and play melodic patterns written in a *do*-centered pentatonic scale (*drm sl d'*).

- Teach *Tideo* by rote. Add pat-clap-snap to each ti-de-o. Transfer it to a pat-clap-partner clap. Create movements for *pass one window* and *jingle at the window*. Perform in a circle with movements and body percussion.

- Display three different numbered *tideo* patterns, as written below. Identify solfege and sing each pattern using solfege syllables and hand signs. Sing through the song. Students identify which pattern they hear, holding up one, two, or three fingers to match the numbered patterns.

- Students move to the barred instruments and play through a full *do*-centered pentatonic scale. Echo-play each *tideo* pattern. Sing the song, playing the *tideo* patterns as they occur in the song.

- After singing and playing the patterns through, ask students questions to lead them to discover some things about the function of notes within *do*-centered pentatonic.
  - Where is the resting or home note? Is it an important note? Why or why not?
  - Which pitches are more important? How do you know?
  - Which pitches are less important? How do you know?

Note: I asked these questions to prepare students for improvising and composing in *do*-pentatonic. We discussed how *do* is important because it is the home note, *so* and *mi* are more important and are used often; *re* and *la* are less important, used mostly as passing or neighbor tones. We also discussed how we didn't use *la* in the three *tideo* patterns we played, but we were singing it.

Students play a *do*-centered pentatonic melody using the text from the poem *Diddle Diddle Dumply*

> Diddle, diddle, dumply.
> Cat is in the plum tree.
> Half a crown to bring her down,
> Diddle, diddle, dumply.

- I created a melody for the poem highlighting the guidelines discussed above. I taught it to the students by echo-playing each measure.

Diddle Diddle Dumply

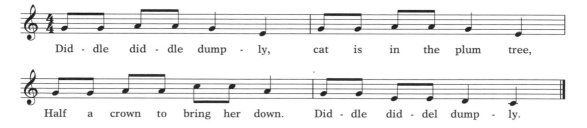

- After students have learned to play the song, ask the following questions:

  1. Does the melody end on the home note?
  2. Does the melody use more of the more important notes, and less of the less important notes?
  3. Does the melody use mostly stepping notes and avoid leaps?

Making Up Music

Students improvise in *do*-centered pentatonic using the poem *Diddle Diddle Dumply*

- Echo-speak the poem, then echo-play the first two measures. Pitches are provided for the first two lines of text (same as from the previous lesson); students will improvise for the remaining two lines of text.

- Working with a partner, students play the first two lines as written above, then improvise the remaining two lines of text. Each time, the teacher provides a new idea for students to incorporate in their improvisations.
  1. End on the home note.
  2. Use more of the more important notes, and less of the less important notes.
  3. Use mostly stepping notes. Avoid leaps.
- Select students to share their improvisation. Assess whether the students followed the general guidelines for playing in *do*-centered pentatonic.

Students play the beginning of *Canon #4* and compose in *do*-centered pentatonic.

- Students echo-play patterns, beginning with the following:

  d' l s

  d' l s

  d' l s m m r d

- Repeat the process, changing the second phrase to match the melody below and improvising during measures three and four.
- After playing through the piece 8–10 times, I asked the students the following questions: *which note did I end on every time? What was I doing during the second half of the piece?* The students figured out that I was improvising and ending on either high or low *do*.
- Working with a partner, students composed measures three and four. They practiced together and shared their compositions at the end of class. Students were evaluated for the following:
  - Did the composition end on the home note? Which one—high or low *do*?
  - Did the composition use all 5 pitches in the *do*-pentatonic scale?
  - Did the composition use more of the more important notes and less of the less important notes?
  - Did the composition use mostly stepping notes and avoid leaps?

Student Examples:

Henry and Olivia

Nathan and Samantha

Angel and Alyssa

- After the students finished sharing, I played the original piece for them. We discussed the same questions I asked them. Note: I adapted the ending from the original so that it would end on *do*, instead of *so*.

Canon #4

Gunild Keetman
adapted by R. Bergeron

- Two classes finished performing this piece with enough time to add a final challenge—playing in canon. I told the students: The title of the piece is *Canon #4*. How would you play this in canon? The composer wanted the canon to start after two beats. Do you think you and your partner could play your piece in canon?
- I selected partners who were confident playing their piece in unison to try playing in canon. Sometimes, I assisted by adding a broken drone.

Making Sense of Music

Students identify melodic phrases in *do*-centered pentatonic.

- As a class, echo-sing melodic phrases from *Tideo* and then read through each of the four different phrases using solfege.

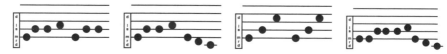

- Individually, match the pattern on the left with the correct solfege on the right.

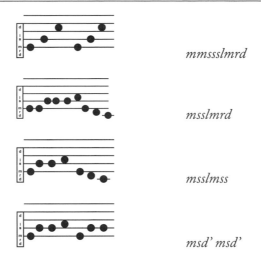

mmssslmrd

msslmrd

msslmss

msd' msd'

Students notate compositions in *do*-centered pentatonic.

- Complete the last two measures by notating your composition from last class. You may work with your partner or alone.

Students reflect on playing, improvising, and composing in *do*-centered pentatonic.

Reflection questions

Why is it called *do*-pentatonic?

Why is the home note important?

Which notes are more important in *do*-pentatonic? Which notes are less important?

When you improvise or compose in *do*-pentatonic, what are two things to remember?

Reflections

I focused on two goals in this unit. I wanted my students to:

1. Discover and understand the roles of the notes in the pentatonic scale.
2. Improvise and compose in *do*-centered pentatonic.

Over the course of the project, I also wanted my students to have ample opportunities to evaluate and reflect on singing and playing in *do*-pentatonic.

Artful

In order to guide students in improvising and composing in *do*-centered pentatonic, I chose to focus on the function of the notes within the *do*-pentatonic scale. However, I didn't want to just tell the students about it; I wanted to lead them to discover which notes were more important, which were less important, and how they were used. To accomplish this, I chose repertoire that had obvious repetition of *so* and *mi*, used *re* and *la* primarily as passing tones or neighbor tones, and had a strong sense of moving toward *do* at the end of a piece.

My students were already familiar with the term "home note" but we hadn't purpose-fully improvised with both high and low *do* before. I chose repertoire that would accent the high do, allowing them opportunities to sing and play high *do* before they composed with it.

Playful

In *Artful-Playful-Mindful*, Jane Frazee uses the term "reflective participation," referring to the goal of "encouraging concentration, exploration, and cooperation in addition to refining ideas and inventing new music." (p. 31) I used *reflective participation* along with the experi-ence of improvising in *do*-pentatonic to prepare students for composition. In my classroom, students often share instruments so they can help each other and learn from each other. At the beginning of this lesson, one partner improvised while the other watched. At the end of each improvisation, the partner who was watching was asked to offer a suggestion or comple-ment. I also provided feedback to the select students who shared their improvisations during class. By allowing opportunities to reflect and offer feedback during the lesson (partner-to-partner and teacher-to-students), I was able to reinforce good strategies for creating melodies in *do*-pentatonic.

Since I was working with eight- and nine-year-olds, I decided it was important to provide enough structure and support to the project in order for them to compose successfully. While I was teaching *Canon #4*, I started simply so that students could echo-play accurately. Stu-dents echoed the first two short phrases each time as written, but on the third longer phrase, I improvised, varying it each time. I established the phrase length that they would be impro-vising by always improvising for seven beats, ending with a rest. Once I established the phrase form, I began playing more complex melodies during the longer phrase.

We practiced the piece together as a class, playing measures one and two as written, and improvising during the last two measures. I guided the improvisations until I felt they were ready to work with a partner. Some classes were ready to work independently sooner than others.

All students were able to compose a final, two-measure phrase, practice it with a partner, and be ready to share at the end of class. Because they already had a beginning to their piece and had improvised several different endings, nobody had trouble getting started or accom-plishing the task.

There were a few compositions that were centered on the top half of the scale ending on high *do* that omitted some of the pentatonic scale notes. In those cases, other students or I made suggestions of how the performers could modify their composition to include the miss-ing notes.

The students were very excited to share their compositions at the end of class. I recorded students' performances using a video camera and used the recordings to further assess their compositions.

Mindful

On day 1 (*Making Music*), we spent a little time looking at staff notation and identifying notes using solfege. We discussed melodic contour, patterns in the music, and the relationship between certain notes. I did this as a review—students had some experience reading *drm sl* patterns on staff—  but I also did this to prepare them for notation and assessment on day 3 (*Making Sense of Music*). On day 3, students reviewed their *Canon #4* compositions at the barred instruments then worked to notate them on the staff. I provided the following visual as a guide, since my students have not had much experience with notating. Since they had worked with a partner on the composition, I allowed them to work together to notate their melody.

Conclusion

I had never taught *do*-pentatonic in this way before, but I believe it was a success. Students seemed to really understand the function of the notes within the scale, and were improvising and composing with this in mind. Even during the first *Playful* exercise, my students were improvising very musical phrases, extending the patterns I had used at the beginning, using *re* as a passing tone, and playing clear endings.

They were also successful in identifying and notating *do*-pentatonic written on the staff. I believe the success with notation came as a result of looking at notation for familiar melodic patterns coupled with a deeper understanding of the *do*-pentatonic scale. Lastly, the project was successful in engaging students. In the end, students had created compositions that they were excited about and proud to share.

Project 10-Smith

Melody Project: *la*-centered pentatonic Grades: 4–5
Repertoire: *I See the Moon* Traditional, adapted by Shelly Smith

Lesson Developer: Shelly Smith

Making Music
Students sing, play, a melody in *la*-centered pentatonic scale

I See the Moon

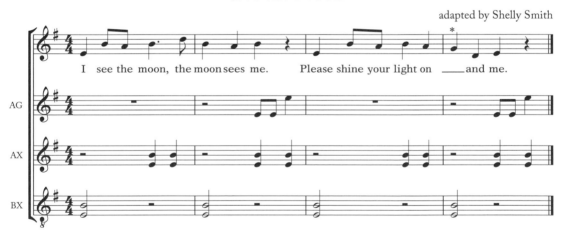

- Introduce the song by filling in the blank (*) with the names of 3–4 students in class. The song is a game in which students take turns being the leader. The class sings the first two measures and the leader finishes the song by filling in the name of a classmate, who becomes the next leader until all have been selected.

- The next time the game is played, add the following body percussion for the BX and AX instrument parts. After having their "turn," students move to play one of the barred instruments. Add the glockenspiel color part as students are able.

Students identify the pitches of the pentatonic scale on the barred instruments and tonal center *la*

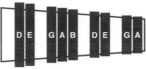

- With all students at the barred instruments, set up in E *la*-centered pentatonic. Students play through the *la*-centered pentatonic scale, beginning and ending on *la* (E). Echo-play a four beat pattern that center in *la*. After the echo play, ask students questions to discover *la* as a tonal center.
    - Where is the resting or home tone in "I See the Moon?" How do you know?
    - What are the other pitches of the song?

Making Up Music

Students improvise melodic patterns in *la*-centered pentatonic

- Brainstorm list of words using a celestial theme:

> Moon, stars, constellations, outer space, sky, "Starry Night,"
> planets, shooting star, space lab, satellites, UFOs, etc.

- Students select words to establish an 8-beat rhythmic structure for melodic improvisation:

- With instruments set up in a E *la*-centered pentatonic scale, invite students to play the entire rhythmic pattern on one note (E). Next give permission to play the pattern on E and a lower or upper neighbor note (D or G). Add A and B on the next two repetitions of the activity. Encourage the students to end their pattern on E. Practice improvising together as a group, then ask for individuals or partner teams to perform for the class.

Making Sense of Music

*Magic Bear**

Materials needed: 7 plastic cups (opaque) and a small stuffed animal that can be hidden under the cup

Line up three cups upside down in front of the class so that all students can see them. (Labeling the cups may be helpful.)

---

* Special thanks to Steve Calantropio for this idea!

Explain that each cup represents one of the pitches they have used in previously learned materials and the game will start with three (*do, re, mi*).

While the children are looking, hide the bear under one of the cups then sing a pattern using all three syllables that ends on the cup covering the animal. Next, ask students to close their eyes and play the game again. (If they need help, you may want to identify the first pitch you will sing.)

I let the students decide when they are ready for the next challenge. (This is usually after 2–3 repetitions of the activity.)

They include:

- Singing patterns on a neutral syllable instead of solfege
- Singing longer patterns
- Adding additional notes (cups) beginning first with low *la* and then finally adding *so* for the entire *la*-centered pentatonic scale.

la,　　　　do　　　re　　　mi　　　so

When they are able, a student becomes the leader. As a leader, my students weren't ready to improvise vocally with accuracy so they played a barred instrument instead. The same rules apply. Start with a limited number of pitches and then expand the game when the kids are ready.

Finally, present the following melodic pattern visuals to the class, explaining that they are part of the melody *I See The Moon*, but that they are out of order. Echo sing through each pattern.

As students make suggestions for changing the order, then sing through all four until the original melody is recreated.

Discuss why the melody is *la*-centered as opposed to *do*-centered.

Reflections

Music Making

The first step in drawing children into this lesson is the element of playing a game. I sing dozens of activities with my lower elementary students using their names. I'm always taken aback by the fact the older children still enjoy the element of surprise when they are selected to be the leader. Oftentimes, this is when I discover a student who seems reluctant to sing matching pitch beautifully!

Making Up

During the second lesson, the children began by reviewing the *I See The Moon* melody first, so they were familiar with *la*-based pentatonic scale before we started improvisation. I know at times I'm guilty of jumping into an improvisation activity too quickly. When children don't have a foundation on where to center their parts, it can be challenging to play in a purposeful way. By starting with the familiar melody and using text derived from a "celestial" theme made them successful during the celestial themed improvisation.

Making Sense

It is my pleasure to report that after spending several sessions using the *APM* model, my students were able to play, improvise and identify the *la* pentatonic scale with confidence. The *Magic Bear* activity has an enormous appeal to the students. It is a simple, yet effective way to reinforce melody concepts and check for understanding. My students have started to make connections between the pieces learned in this lesson as well as previously learned material. One of the most satisfying moments was watching children who seem reluctant to take risks become more confident in their ability to demonstrate their musical skills.

Project 11-Davis

Melody Project: *re*-centered pentatonic   Grades: 6–7

Repertoire: *Instrumental Piece II Discovering Keetman*, #12, p. 33

Shady Grove, Appalachian folk song

Lesson Developer: Leonard Davis

Making Music

Students play through all the pentatonic modes and tonal centers by using patterns derived from poem *One for Ice Cream*

- Working alone or with partners (depending on class size and number of barred instruments available) students set up barred instruments in C pentatonic. Students revisit and remember a familiar poem from music class (with a variation according to my students' home state, of course).

Jane Frazee
Discovering Orff

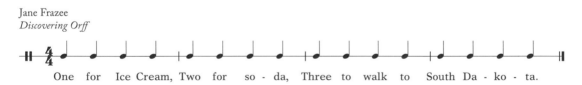

One for   Ice Cream, Two for   so - da,   Three to   walk   to   South Da - ko - ta.

- Let's play our entire poem on C. Now let's find a way to play *One for Ice Cream* up the scale (C-D-E-G). Let's start on A and walk back down for *Two for Soda* (A-G-E-D). Let's play the first pattern for *Three to walk to* and you find a way to get back to C at the end of South Dakota.

One for   Ice Cream, Two for   so - da,   Three to   walk   to   ta.

- Let's use the melody with your variation and start one note up! What pitch did we start on? (D) What pitch did we end on? (D) What would it sound like if we started on E? (Students play) Start on G? (Students play) Start on A? (Students play) Let's go back to the starting note D. (Students play) If C is *do*-centered pentatonic, what would a home tone of D be? That's right, our *Ice Cream* poem melody is in re-pentatonic!

Students play *Instrumental Piece II* (*Discovering Keetman*, #12, p. 33) on the barred instruments.

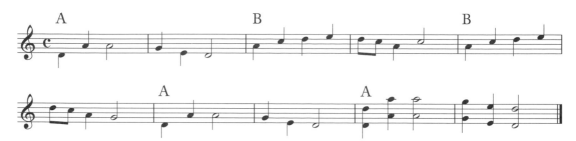

- I started first by playing the entire piece for my students so that they got the melody into their ears. I played the melody alone a few times to draw their attention to the form (ABBA), the melodic contour of each phrase and how the melodic line is centered on *re*. Students learned to play the first phrase through echo imitation by playing and singing the letter names. The first phrase was simple enough for all students to master after one or two tries. We then identified the first phrase as our A phrase and I had the students play the A phrase (beginning and ending) while I played the B phrase/middle section alone. Most of the students were able to master this the first time. Students echo played the B patterns and we briefly noted how the first B melody went back up to C and the second B pattern went down to G. We then put all of the parts together. Students worked on playing the additional A phrase in octaves. I then gave additional time so that students could work alone or with their partners on the entire melody before we brought it back together to play a few final times. This gave me a chance to work individually with a few students that had troubles with the middle section and for students to help each other out. I accompanied the students with a bordun (D and A) on the bass xylophone as they played together. A few students wanted to play alone and in small groups to demonstrate that they had mastered it.

Students sing and/or listen to an Appalachian folk song in re-pentatonic.

- I saved this experience for the end of music class for a closing activity. I introduced the song by singing alone and accompanying on the Autoharp. Once I sang the melody two or three times, I invited my students to join along. Students were able to immediately participate in the memorable melody. If there was remaining time in the class, students listened to and watched a YouTube video of Jean Ritchie performing *Shady Grove*.

Making Up Music

Students explore the *re*-pentatonic mode though free improvisation on the barred instruments.

- Working alone or with partners (depending on class size and number of barred instruments available) students set up barred instruments in C pentatonic. Students can begin by echo playing patterns played by teacher that are centered in *re*/D, perhaps patterns derived from *Instrumental Piece II*. Students are then given time to freely improvise, with the only requirement that their improvisations return to the *re* home tone. Encourage the students to keep their rhythms simple and focus mostly on creating interesting melodic lines centered on *re*.

Students create questions and answers in AB form.
- A time for free improvisation flows naturally into creating question and answer phrases. Students can work alone to create both their own question and answer or can work with a partner in creating together two contrasting phrases. The teacher has the opportunity to listen and watch student exploration, pointing out to the class student ideas that can serve as different possibilities.
- A successful experience has been asking students, who haven't been working together but have unknowingly created contrasting phrases, to come together and combine their ideas into a melody. For example, during this portion of the lesson, Preston and Jonah created the following ideas that could work together.

Preston (A)   Jonah (B)

Students compose a barred instrument melody in *re*-pentatonic, using elemental form.
- Using student ideas like Preston and Jonah's, the class can play with different possibilities for a melody that uses elemental form. Students discover that some choices, like those ending with the B phrase or an A phrase that does not end with a D, are less likely to feel like the melody is centered in *re*-pentatonic.

- Students are given the task to create a melody with two contrasting sections that uses elemental form. Students create an A phrase and a B phrase, choose a form, put together, and then share their work with the rest of the class.

Form	
AAAB	AABB
ABAA	ABAB
ABBB	ABBA

Student Examples:

Jonah and Preston

Ariel

Making Sense of Music

Students notate their *re*-pentatonic melodies.

- The *Playful* week transitions seamlessly into *Mindful* week work by allowing the students the opportunity to finish their compositions by notating them. There are a variety of ways for students to notate, from traditional staff paper and pencil to notation programs using computers. I gave my students to option of either using paper and pencil or using *NotateMe* (app for iOS devices) to notate their compositions. Some of my students began this work at the end of the *Playful* lesson from last week because they had completed their ideas. Notating the projects took about 25–30 minutes of class time.

Student examples:

Students analyze melodies in *re*-pentatonic.

- Individuals or pairs of students were given the chance to perform their melody for the rest of the class. It quickly became a game to see who could identify the form of their peers' instrumental piece! In addition to identifying the form, I was able to facilitate group discussion and reflection by asking a few of the following questions with my students after each performance:

- How was *re* as a home tone used? How were the A and B sections the same? How were they different? How does *re* as a home tone affect the mood and feel of the piece? How do you think the piece would sound with an accompaniment on the bass xylophone? Were there repeated patterns in the piece? Did the melody move mostly in repeated notes, steps, skips, etc.? What was the range of the piece? How would the mood change it were played on a different instrument or at a slower/faster tempo? Do you think that we could play this melody in canon? Why? Why not?

Reflections

When I first began to develop this project, I turned to *Orff-Schulwerk: Applications for the Classroom* by Brigitte Warner. Chapter 8 of the book is devoted to the pentatonic modes and was rich in theoretical and background information on the modes with ideas for classroom application. There were two quotes from the book that I used to guide myself in developing a project for *re*-pentatonic.

The first quote gave me inspiration to develop this project working backwards, starting first with *Mindful* week and then moving to *Playful* and *Artful* weeks:

> In regards to pentatonic modes, the teacher must decide where the priorities lie and what knowledge and skills need to be taught in order to build a firm foundation for future development. [2]

With this and the "less is more" mantra in mind, I decided that this project priority would be that my students could create for themselves a melody that was centered in *re* and that used elemental form and that they could articulate how their melody worked as a *re*-pentatonic example.

The second quote was concerned with time and getting my students to understand how the modes worked in melody:

> Our most time consuming task will be to familiarize the children with the sound essences of the various modes as they manifest themselves, not through scale patterns, but through melody. [3]

I began first with my students playing patterns based on *One for Ice Cream* so that they could visually and aurally distinguish between different tonal centers. A brief introduction to all of the modes this way will help students with future projects using the other modes (*mi, sol, la*) as well. But, as Warner suggested, the most time would need to be spent on learning by playing, learning by creating, and learning by analyzing and reflection how *re*-centered pentatonic works.

With the *Mindful* and overall project goal decided upon, I wanted to select pieces that would be beautiful examples of *re*-centered pentatonic. I felt like this pentatonic project could be a marriage of the Keetman barred instrument world and the rich world of American Appalachian folk songs. I decided upon using one of the barred instrument pieces that Frazee suggested in *APM*, and *Shady Grove*, a well-known Appalachian folk song. *Shady Grove* is one of my favorite *re*-pentatonic melodies; I just love the rhythmic vitality and the mood that the *re* tonal center creates. My students' classes really enjoyed the song and were mesmerized by the YouTube clip of Jean Ritchie performing with a lap dulcimer. When I asked them why they found the video so intriguing, they answered that they had never seen or heard anything like this before. It is true—the modes sound foreign at first to the ears of my pop-centric students.

For *Playful* work, I knew that this upper age level of students was ready to completely take ownership of their creative process. Because these students have been working with me for a number of years, they have had considerable experience with barred instrument improvisation, creating question and answer phrases, and using elemental form, I knew that they were capable of creating pieces that were all their own, yet inspired by the Keetman piece. My students had a chance to freely improvise and experiment with creating question and answer phrases, but the majority of the time was spent working independently to create a melody modeled after *Instrumental Piece II*. My role became that of the coach circulating amongst the different groups around the room, listening to where they were at in the process and to ask questions so that they could articulate the why of the musical choices they were making and to get them to consider other possibilities if they were stuck.

Giving my students the opportunity to notate their melodies was for me a *Mindful* week endeavor because it was another chance to see if students could read and write patterns on the staff and also gave them visible evidence of their learning: written out music that they created for themselves and that they could go home and share. Notating and writing can take large amounts of time for students to complete successfully, but I decided for this project that the time was worth it so that my students could have tangible and visual evidence of their learning in class. Our compositions hung on the wall outside the music room for a few weeks to show the rest of the school before they were sent home with students.

Project 12-Larsen

Melody Project: Dorian Mode   Grades: 6–7

Repertoire: *Andante III, Music for Children*, Vol. IV, p. 46, #3
Lesson Developer: Diana Larsen

Making Music

Students perform a melody in Dorian mode on barred instruments.

- *I am going to play a short melody on my recorder. Using your fingertips, find the four notes on your barred instrument. When you've figured it out, raise your hand and show me how to play it.*
- Teacher plays; students learn by rote.

- After most of the class has found the motif on their instruments, I notice Sophia has found the matching pitches. *Let's listen and watch Sophia play. On which note does she begin? And what's the final note? That's right—D. Who can tell me on which notes do most of the pieces we have learned in music class start and end? C or A. So, this is something new. We'll talk more about that later. Now let's learn the rest of this melody.*
- *What does it sound like twice in a row?*

- *Now, I'm going to make a change. Listen carefully.*

- *What's different? Right, we play the second high D twice. Ready for the next challenge? Here goes!* Teacher plays:

- *What did I change this time? Yes, the B changed to B-C.*
- *OK. We're well on our way! You play what you know, and I'm going to add something new.* Students play the first two measures, then the teacher sings measures three and four with lyrics, "Something else will go right here." Students discover the melody ascends stepwise from the high D, then jumps to low G and walks down to low D.

Some-thing else will go right here

- *OK. I think you've got this! Let's take a moment to analyze this melody. What's our home tone again? Right, D. On our barred instruments with the regular set up—no F-sharps or B-flats—a melody with home tone D that uses all seven pitches is in Dorian mode. Over the next couple of weeks, we're going to get used to this mode's special sound, compose in this mode, and even learn to recognize it by ear. What's this mode called again? Dorian!*

- *Let's take a minute to think of our melody in terms of numbers. On which number do we begin the tune? Let's try singing the whole melody with numbers—8 67 5 1 88 67 5 1 1' 2' 3' 4 3 2 1*
- *What would it sound like if we shifted our pitch set down one note? Let's try it! How would you describe this sound? What do you notice? Pitch number 3 sounds different—a little higher—and pitch 7 also sounds a little higher. Why would that be? On our instruments, all of the bars are equally spaced. Why does it sound different?*
- *Follow me to the piano. I want to show you how this melody transfers to the piano keys.* Teacher plays the melody starting on D, then plays it again starting on C, using all white keys. *What do you notice? Which keys did I not use? Right, the black keys!* Teacher plays melody on the piano starting on C, using E-flat and B-flat. *But on our barred instruments, we're going to stick with home tone D; I just wanted you to see if you could figure out how our barred instruments are different than a piano.*

- *So, remind me, what's the name of this mode we're exploring? That's right – DORIAN mode.*

Making Up Music

Students compose a new way to play the final eight beats of a sixteen-beat melody in Dorian mode.

- *Last week we learned a melody in Dorian mode. The beginning of the melody sounded like this (play measures 1 and 2) and the end sounded like this (play measures 3 and 4). This week we're going to toss out the ending so you can reinvent the melody in a different way.*
  - *Let's look at the notation on the SmartBoard. How many beats will be available for your new ending?*

Checklist
- Uses all pitches: D E F G A B C (D)
- Ends on home tone D
- Changes
  - rhythm
  - meldoy
  - both

  - *Part of what makes this a modal melody is that it uses all pitches of the scale. Which pitches do you need to make sure to include in your new ending? Right, pitches 2, 3 and 4 (E, F and G). All of the other notes are covered in measures 1 and 2.*
  - *And on which note must the melody end? Yes, D.*
  - *The composer of the original melody brings the tune into a higher octave in the third measure; you can do that if you like, or bring it down into the lower octave right away. The composer uses mostly quarter notes in the final two measures. You can use notes of longer or shorter duration. The composer didn't use any rests. You can if you like. Let me play you a few ideas before you get to work.*
  - *While it may seem that the main point of this task is to come up with a fabulous new ending to this melody, what I really want you to do is get the sound of Dorian mode in your ear. Think about this—if I were to play a tune at the end of class (or next week), would you recognize the special sound of this mode? What makes it sound different than other music we have experience together in the music room?*
  - *Enjoy your time playing in Dorian mode!*

- Students work alone or in small groups to compose an ending to the phrase. After the teacher gives work time and provides individual support as needed, students perform for each other while the teacher (or student) video records performances to include in a digital portfolio.

Examples include:

Making Sense of Music

Students demonstrate understanding of Dorian mode by 1) identifying examples as Dorian/ not Dorian, 2) explaining how modal melodies differ when played on barred instruments and a piano, and 3) describing the sound of Dorian mode in their own words.

- Teacher plays several examples on piano or recorder, and students identify the mode as *Dorian* or *not Dorian*.

Making Sense of Music | Dorian | Name _____

What do you hear? Circle your answer.

	a)	b)
1.	Dorian mode	non Dorian mode
	a)	b)
2.	Dorian mode	non Dorian mode
	a)	b)
3.	Dorian mode	non Dorian mode

- For question one, the teacher plays the original melody. Answer: Dorian mode

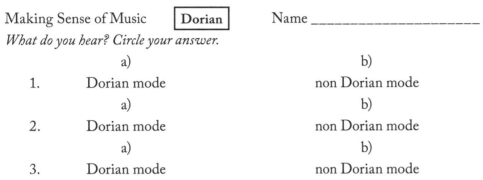

- For question two, the teacher plays the original melody transposed down a step. Will the students understand that this is still Dorian mode even though it is pitched lower? Answer: Dorian mode

- For the final listening question, the first half of the melody sounds the same, but the teacher checks to see if students notice a change in the final two measures, as the F-natural becomes an F-sharp. Answer: not Dorian mode

- Then students compare playing modal melodies on barred instruments and the piano.
    4. *To play in Dorian mode on our barred instruments we must always start on D, but on a piano we could start on any key. Why? What does a piano have that our xylophones do not?*
- Then students explain subjectively how a musical mode might suggest a mood, using the example of film scores as a writing prompt.
    5. *If your Dorian melody accompanied a scene in a movie, what would be happening on screen? What type of movie would it be? A mystery, romantic comedy, horror or something different? Why?*

6. Why do you think movie directors hire composers to write music for their movies? What does music add to the viewing experience?

Reflections

As I began planning this project, I set out to create a meaningful experience for my sixth graders that could leave them with more language to talk about their experiences. My sixth graders flourish when given the time to solve musical problems. My challenge was to imbed critical thinking tasks within their music-making experiences.

After selecting a 16-beat Dorian melody (*Andante III* from *Music for Children*, Vol. IV, p. 46 #3) I made a conscious decision to leave out the ostinato and playful B section for a performance later in the year. I developed a process for teaching that melody that asked students to identify subtle changes as they listened and analyzed my playing. This repetition allowed everyone to become familiar with the sound of Dorian mode.

I also realized that if I wanted my students to identify melodies as Dorian, they would need to compare this new concept to something they know well—Ionian mode. When I realized some students didn't understand why melodies sound different depending on which pitch they begin on a xylophone, I determined that my somewhat sophisticated sixth graders needed a mini compare-and-contrast lesson at the piano.

I didn't take too long explaining the Making Up Music task; they are old pros at this type of composition activity. It's for this reason I took the time to point out the main objective of the project, "to get the sound of Dorian mode in your ear." I was curious if this would affect how they approached their creative task. Needless to say, I was excited about many of their melodies. I noticed many students used rhythm figures they had learned in 4th and 5th grade and found interesting ways to orchestrate arrangements in pairs and small groups. Other years I would have been pleased with their compositions and wrapped up the unit with performances of their compositions, but I knew I wanted to dig deeper; they needed to talk about the sound of this new mode. I was curious to observe if they would regurgitate my words or bring their own voices into their explanations.

In the assessment I put together, the first three questions are objective: is this Dorian or not? Right or wrong. I knew if they got all three correct, they likely got it. With one or more wrong, they may be able to talk about Dorian mode all day, but the aural identification part was still in development. That's OK—it's just helpful to know this information to guide future instruction. Initially I planned to use different melodies in the first three questions, but I decided to come back to slight variations on the original tune. As I reviewed their answers, I observed that most students heard the major third in question three and marked "not Dorian mode," yet many students chose the incorrect answer for question two. This suggests they confused the concepts of mode and pitch. Next time I would consider adding a listening game at the beginning of the third week to practice listening for these subtle changes.

In questions four, five and six I wanted to give my students the opportunity to write more freely and subjectively. I knew if I asked "How would you describe this new sound?" that would be too abstract for many of my students. By linking the mood it projects to a movie genre, I thought students might write with less inhibition. Some student responses were quite insightful:

Examples:

4. To play in Dorian mode on our barred instruments we must always start on D, but on a piano we could start on any key. Why? What does a piano have that our xylophones do not?

   ○ *A piano has black keys. They can be used for in-between notes. A xylophone doesn't have in-between notes, like a piano!*—Alyssa

   ○ *Sharps and flats, although technically you can get sharps and flats on a xylophone by switching the bars.*—Reece

5. If your Dorian melody accompanied a scene in a movie, what would be happening on screen? What type of movie would it be? A mystery, romantic comedy, horror or something different? Why?

   ○ *A mystery, because at first it seems like it's a normal day, then something mysterious happens.*—Ann

   ○ *Like an adventure movie. I can imagine a person going off to something or someone.*—Abby

   ○ *Horror, because the piece sounds like a ghost coming at you in slow motion.*—Eden

   ○ *A mystery because it sounds like something that would be played on an organ that had no player.*—Jaymeson

   ○ *I think a mystery, and a girl who finds out she's a ghost girl is running away from her fears because of the tone of the Dorian melody.*—Caroline

6. Why do you think movie directors hire composers to write music for their movies? What does music add to the viewing experience?

   ○ *It adds another atmosphere that makes the movie better or worse. Movie directors hire composes because they can't write music and they need someone who knows about music.*—Ann

   ○ *The music gives a feel for the situation you or the characters are in.*—Alyssa

   ○ *Music adds a little more suspense and magic to the movie.*—Elena

   ○ *Music adds to the viewing experience in different ways. Music can add to a horror film in creating an eerie feeling while in an action movie it could give a fight feeling. Music is a very important attribute in movies.*—Caitlyn

   ○ *Because music adds a sense of feeling. A scary part doesn't feel very scary without music.*—Reece

Sixth and seventh graders are at a unique stage in their personal and intellectual development. A well-designed *APM* lesson gives them a much-needed structure counterbalanced with periods of autonomy. And perhaps most importantly, the Project Model insists that both the students and the teacher pay attention to how a student makes sense of their musical experience. Master of the middle school general music classroom, Jo Ella Hug suggests:

> Under the guidance of an experienced and secure Orff-Schulwerk teacher, students can leave middle school with unique abilities. They have the raw materials to become independent learners. They have basic knowledge on which to frame advancing skills as abstract thinking becomes the norm. And they have a good understanding of the internal structure of music.

Conclusion

Artistry, therefore, can serve as a regulative ideal for education, a vision that adumbrates what really matters in schools. To conceive of students as artists who do their art in science, in the arts, or the humanities, is, after all, both a daunting and a profound aspiration. It may be that by shifting the paradigm of education reform and teaching from one modeled after the clocklike character of the assembly line into one that is closer to the studio or innovative science laboratory might provide us with a vision that better suits the capacities and the futures of the students we teach. It is in this sense, I believe, that the field of education has much to learn from the arts about the practice of education. It is time to embrace a new model for improving our schools. [1]

—Elliot Eisner

When we picked up *Artful–Playful–Mindful* in 2012 we knew right away we had stumbled upon something special. In Jane Frazee's latest contribution to the Orff-Schulwerk landscape, we found a framework for teaching music that charges teachers to provide something beyond experiential learning for their students. Frazee's words—"We all learn by doing, but we can learn even more by examining what we have done " [2]—resonated with us. Her vision integrated the beauty of Orff-Schulwerk into a framework that shifts the instructional focus from performance to a balance of making, making up and making sense of music. And what really sealed the deal was that we could envision how this approach would play out in our real-world classrooms. Now, after experimenting with the Project Model at several grade levels over the last three years, we have come to think of *APM* as an expanded vision of Orff-Schulwerk retooled for a new generation of learners.

When we began implementing the Project Model in our work with children, we noticed a remarkable change in our classrooms. Our students started answering and asking more questions. This examination of new concepts became possible when students acquired language introduced during artful week, used it as they worked cooperatively on a playful task, and again as they articulated their learning during mindful culminating activities. And this dynamic conversation helped our students start to see music class as more than a place to sing new songs or play fun pieces; the students began to see themselves as collaborators in a joyful music-learning laboratory—a studio—where they were both the creators and critics.

This shift from classroom to studio changes the role of the teacher as well. During week one, the teacher's role is primarily that of musician, modeling musicianship in both the choice of materials and in performance. This is how students become expressive musicians – by emulating their teachers! In the second week, the teacher becomes coach, providing differentiated support to students to help them clarify their thinking as they make musical choices. And in week three, the teacher is a skillful facilitator, guiding students to reflect upon and construct meaning in response to their own and others' work.

Retooling Orff-Schulwerk for the 21st century demands that we examine not only what we ask from our students but also from ourselves as music educators. We believe that challenging ourselves as musicians and pedagogues—as we have attempted with our *APM* work—is a worthy endeavor for all professionals and one that is well within the grasp of every trained music teacher. Because the Orff-Schulwerk approach offers a rich variety of stimulating activities (singing, saying, dancing and playing) to discover the essence of music, it is a perfect source for *APM* explorations.

And what may be especially notable about our experiment in *APM* is that we undertook it on our own. No committee, administrator or governing body said we had to do it. In a time when society seems increasingly concerned with what and how children learn to read and do math, music educators continue to look for professional guidance and leadership from within our own community. So instead of waiting around for someone to tell us what to do, we sought out our own professional learning community to improve the quality of music instruction in our classrooms. We took on *APM* to help our students learn about their own thinking and learning processes. We continue to strive to develop meaningful music lessons that integrate creativity, critical thinking, communication and collaboration. By doing this work, we show the broader community that music deserves a place on the 21st-century education stage. Frazee adds, "Wouldn't you like to tell the world that you and your students do all of these things in a medium that touches the heart as well as the mind?" [3]

Orff-Schulwerk has provided a half-century of musical discoveries for students and their teachers. *APM* now builds on this successful foundation to help students to discover the delight of understanding—as well as making—music. As public school music teachers who have found new enthusiasm and commitment for our work, we hope that our successes working with this model can become your own. This book is a testament to the professional growth that awaits you!

You are doing great human work. May it reward and sustain you through a long and fulfilling career. [4]

References

Introduction

1. Frazee, Jane, *Artful-Playful-Mindful: A New Orff-Schulwerk Curriculum for Music Making and Music Thinking*. New York: Schott Music Corp., 2012, p. 22.

2. Ibid, pp. 1–2.

3. Larsen, D. (accessed 2014, August 7). *What is Orff-Schulwerk?* [Video file]. http://aosa.org/about/what-is-orff-schulwerk/

4. Calantropio, Steven: *Process Teaching: Finding the Elements*, *Orff Echo*, Vol. 36, No. 4 (Summer 2004), p. 28.

5. Frazee, Jane, *APM*, p. 20.

6. Frazee, Jane: *Orff Schulwerk Today*, New York: Schott Music Corp., 2006, p. 105.

7. Frazee, Jane, *APM*, p. 20.

Part 1
Rhythm Projects
Grades 2–3

 Mouse, Mousie — Traditional

#20, Keetman — *Erstes Spiel am Xylophon*, p. 12

Lizard in My Soup — K. Benson

Listen to the Sun — *Music for Children* (Am.ed), II, p. 191

Who's That Tapping at the Window? — *APM*, p. 55

1. Frazee, Jane, *Orff Schulwerk Today*. New York: Schott, 2006, pp. 141–142.

Grades 4–5

 Alabama Gal — *APM*, p. 57

Dance Josey — *Discovering Orff*, p. 155

Ding Dong, Diggidiggidong — *Music For Children*, I, p. 24

1. Frazee, Jane, *Artful-Playful-Mindful: A New Orff-Schulwerk Curriculum for Music Making and Music Thinking*. New York: Schott, 2012, p. 10.

2. Ibid, p. 18.

Grades 6–7

♫♩	Old Betty Larkin	folk song
Bubblegum, Bubblegum	Traditional, LD adaptation
Musette in D	J.S. Bach
♩.♪	Bats Eat Bananas
(Khaang *Khaaw Kin* Kluay)	Thai Traditional

1. Spurgeon, Alan L., *Waltz the Hall: The American Play Party*. University Press of Mississippi, 2008.

2. Frazee, Jane, *Artful-Playful-Mindful: A New Orff-Schulwerk Curriculum for Music Making and Music Thinking*. New York: Schott Music Corp., 2012, p. 22.

Part 2
Melody Projects
Grades 2–3

d-r-m	#12, *Erstes Spiel am Xylophon*, p. 9	Gunild Keetman
Hot Spicy Tacos/Hot Cross Buns	Traditional, KB adaptation
Carillon from *L'Arlésienne Suite No. 1*	Georges Bizet
d-r-m-s	Spielstucke #8	*Discovering Keetman*, p. 11

1. Frazee, Jane, *Artful-Playful-Mindful: A New Orff-Schulwerk Curriculum for Music Making and Music Thinking*. New York: Schott, 2012, p. 1.

Grades 4–5

d-r-m-s-l-d'	Tideo	folk song
Diddle Diddle Dumply	*Exploring Orff*, p. 164
Canon #4	*Music For Children*, I, p. 91
la-centered pentatonic	I See the Moon	Traditional, SS adaptation

1. Frazee, Jane, *Artful-Playful-Mindful: A New Orff-Schulwerk Curriculum for Music Making and Music Thinking*. New York: Schott Music Corp., 2012, p. 31.

Grades 6–7

re-centered pentatonic	Instrumental Piece II	*Discovering Keetman* #12, p. 33
Shady Grove	Appalachian folk song
Dorian mode	Andante III	*Music For Children*, IV, p. 46

1. Jean Ritchie, *Shady Grove* [video file]. https://www.youtube.com/watch?v=pDUNdRm5Toc

2. Warner, Brigitte: *Orff-Schulwerk Applications for the Classroom*, Englewood Cliffs, NJ: Prentice-Hall, 1991, p. 199.

3. Hug, JoElla: Course notes for Orff in the Middle School Classroom, University of St. Thomas, July 15–19, 2013.

Conclusion

1. Smith, M. K. (2005) "Elliot W. Eisner, connoisseurship, criticism and the art of education," the encyclopaedia of informal education, www.infed.org/thinkers/eisner.htm.

2. Frazee, Jane: *Artful-Playful-Mindful*, New York: Schott Music Corp., 2012, p. vi.

3. Frazee, Jane. Improvisation Panel, AOSA November 8 2014.

4. Frazee, Jane: *Orff Schulwerk Today*, New York: Schott Music Corp., 2006, p. 230.